STUDIES IN ENGLISH LITERATURE

Volume XLIX

HOFFMAN, Stanton DeVoren. **Comedy and Form in the Fiction of Joseph Conrad.** Mouton (dist. by Humanities), 1969. 140p (Studies in English Literature, 49) 69-29628. 6.50

CHOICE   MAR. '70
Language & Literature
English & American

A somewhat misleading title because Hoffman is not essentially interested in comic form. The book consists of three essays, two long ones on *Heart of Darkness* and *Lord Jim* followed by a potpourri on "Youth," "Falk," "The Return," "An Outpost of Progress," *The Secret Agent*, and *Victory*. In each essay, the words "low comedy," "farce," "burlesque," and "slapstick" recur frequently and appropriately in reference to details of characterization or behavior, but in no case do they describe comedy as an important *structure* of the works being examined. By identifying comedy with the grotesque, Hoffman stakes out false claims for comedy when he is really talking about ironic structures. One sentence about his best case, "Youth," illustrates these theoretical confusions: "Every moment and every movement of youth's illusion and romance and the romantic self is checked by anti-romance and a reality which is the antithesis of romance (made comic to show this clearly — comedy is then one of the poles of the conflict within Marlow between illusion and reality, between romance and anti-romance, but since it is the basic reality, the conflict seems to be re-

Continued

HOFFMAN

CHOICE   MAR. '70
Language & Literature
English & American

solved in terms of victory, and comedy's function is to obtain this victory and double purgation)." (p. 104) Apart from stylistic ineptness, which is unfortunately characteristic of the book as a whole, such juggling of terms tells us very little about "Youth." There are some fine insights buried in the essays on *Heart of Darkness* and *Lord Jim*, but they have only marginal relevance to comedy. Not recommended.

COMEDY AND FORM
IN THE FICTION
OF
JOSEPH CONRAD

by

STANTON DE VOREN HOFFMAN

Sir George Williams University

1969

MOUTON

THE HAGUE · PARIS

LIBRARY OF CONGRESS CATALOG CARD NUMBER: 69-29628

Printed in The Netherlands by Mouton & Co., Printers, The Hague

For
Howard and Martha

ACKNOWLEDGMENTS

The author wishes to express gratitude to Professors Robert Frank and Bruce Sutherland of the Pennsylvania State University, who read this book in its preliminary form, an earlier version having been completed under the auspices of the graduate school of that university. He further wishes to express gratitude to *Studies in Short Fiction* and the *Ball State University Forum* for having kindly granted permission to reprint the sections of the chapters on *Heart of Darkness* and *Lord Jim* which appeared as essays in those journals, and to Sir George Williams University for, in part, having made the publication of this study possible. Mr. Claude St. Onge and Miss Judith Lonn provided valuable assistance in the preparation of the final manuscript of this study.

TABLE OF CONTENTS

I

INTRODUCTION

General observations on and amazement about the progress of
Conrad criticism, especially that of the last ten or fifteen years,
are almost commonplace in any study which has pretensions of
viewing itself as another step in this progress. The amazement is
justified. A writer of the sea and of the traditional values of order
and profession has become a darker voice in a wilderness, but more
than that, he has become the artist carefully creating a whole out
of a vast array of elements, moulding form with symbols, with
images, with recurring motifs and patterns, with various languages
and styles. Moral dimensions are modified by ontological ones.
Conrad's concerns are how shall a man be, transcending as well
as including questions of how he shall know, feel, and act. These
things are often seen in the light of encounters with the self.[1]
Conrad has a great vision of disorder and anarchy, and of the corrupting forces which create this chaos. The feeling is, according
to one critic, that Conrad's novels are "profound parables of moral
struggle containing recurrent patterns of symbolism and reference",[2] and, most recently, several of Conrad's most important
characters have become defined in terms of being and self brought
to their very limits, with a confrontation of futility and isolation
and hopelessness and the recognition of the necessity of acting out
commitment.[3]

[1] See the work of Albert J. Guerard.
[2] Vernon Young, "Joseph Conrad: Outline for a Reconsideration", *Hudson
Review*, II (1949), 7.
[3] See Murray Krieger's *The Tragic Vision* (New York, 1960) and the article

There has been examination of the villains of several of Conrad's novels — men like the captain or second engineer of the *Patna* in *Lord Jim*, or like the accountant or the manager's uncle or the man with the black moustaches in *Heart of Darkness*, or Martin Ricardo or Schomberg in *Victory* — characters that have been called caricatures and grotesques. One critic has said that, "Conrad drew his villains black ... because he intended them to embody moral evil so plainly that they could be distinguished from the fully human characters in his later tales."[4] Another has remarked — and it should be noted that Conrad's villains are quite black and over-simplified in his earlier works also — that Conrad made these characters into grotesques in order to obtain a kind of fictional reality "that the flat and commonplace seldom attains", to create intense visual and dramatic surprise.[5] There is more to it than this. A few critics, in the form of hints, have made the proper observation. Hewitt, for instance, in speaking about *Lord Jim*, has written that Jim's crime "is described in terms which are reminiscent of some passages of 'Heart of Darkness' — in terms of what, in that story, is called 'sordid farce'", and also, "there is a flavour of shameless farce about all the weaknesses and crimes of which Conrad writes at this time; his mean characters are all horribly comic."[6] He does not say why. Another critic, Haugh, similarly saw a comic opera aspect to parts of the presentation of the *Patna's* captain, and saw him as basically portrayed as a clown.[7] The comic in Conrad has been noted elsewhere. In the *Secret Agent* an element of this same brutal and sordid farce is dominant, and the novel is "more nearly a comedy than any other novel of Conrad".[8] In this same novel there is "rich moral comedy", "macabre comedy", "chill humor", and specific comic situations and characters.[9]

---

by C. N. Starvou, "Conrad, Camus, and Sisyphus", *Audience*, VII (1960), 80-96.

[4] Paul Wiley, *Conrad's Measure of Man* (Madison, Wisconsin, 1954), p. 147.

[5] Albert J. Guerard, *Conrad the Novelist* (Cambridge, Mass., 1958), p. 174.

[6] See his *Conrad: A Reassessment* (Philadelphia, 1952), p. 32.

[7] See his *Joseph Conrad, Discovery in Design* (Norman, Oklahoma, 1957), p. 64.

[8] Hewitt, p. 85.

[9] Guerard, *Conrad the Novelist*, p. 219, p. 227, p. 230.

And *Heart of Darkness* suggests a "lunatic asylum".[10] *The Shadow Line* suggests that Conrad "often gives a split ironic vision to deathly events with the comic or ludicrous posed simultaneously",[11] and in *Chance*, "the taste of Fyne for excursions returns as a *leitmotiv* and gives constancy to this personage, half burlesqued, half serious".[12]

All Conrad's mean characters are "horribly comic". Marlow, in at least two of Conrad's major works, tells us as much, when he makes reference to "sordid farce" and "lugubrious drollery" in *Heart of Darkness*, and to "burlesque meanness" in *Lord Jim*. Speaking of Jim and the abandonment of the *Patna*, Marlow notes that Jim "enjoyed the privilege of witnessing scenes — as far as I can judge — of low comedy";[13] and he soon adds, "... there was an element of burlesque in his ordeal — a degradation of funny grimaces in the approach of death or dishonour".[14] It shall be the contention of the following chapters that this burlesque or farce or low comedy is present to some considerable and puzzling degree. And it is present for what appear to be certain fairly well-defined purposes, purposes that can be best revealed when this comic element is considered in terms of everything else that is happening in the novels and tales in which it appears.

Marlow makes reference to burlesque in *Lord Jim* and to farce in *Heart of Darkness*, and his reference is to the behaviour and descriptions of the officers in the former, and to the activity of the "pilgrims" in the latter. Elsewhere we find people making statements in backgrounds and places which negate these statements; we find knockabout clowning and considerable slapstick.[15] What is

[10] F. R. Leavis, *The Great Tradition* (London, 1948), p. 176.
[11] Haugh, p. 84.
[12] Irene Simon, *Formes du roman anglais de Dickens a Joyce* (Liege, 1949), p. 271.
[13] *Lord Jim* (New York, 1931, Modern Library), p. 101. All subsequent quotations and references to this novel will be to this edition.
[14] *Ibid.*, p. 105. This ninth chapter is filled with reference to "knockabout clowns in a farce", "comic business", "new capers", "new antics", etc.
[15] Bergson's definition can be applied here. In his essay "On Laughter", he saw the comic in terms of the mechanical, the rigid, and the dehumanized. "The attitudes, gestures and movements of the human body are laughable in exact proportion as that body reminds us of a mere machine." The movement of farce is the mechanical, and it sets before us the "obvious clockwork arrange-

to follow is to have as its concern something called burlesque or farce by Marlow and some critics, and something quite commonly and traditionally recognized as such. I wish to suggest that this type of comedy occurs with some frequency in certain specific situations and types of works, and that it occurs with enough frequency to raise questions concerning its existence in contexts where it must seem initially disturbing. The contexts of the novels and stories in which this comic element appears seem to work heavily against any such element, and especially against its recognition and functioning. It is my feeling that this low comedy, in these contexts, is to be viewed as a metaphor perhaps functioning as a metaphor amongst metaphors. And one could entitle a paper on this subject, not only "The Prevalency of Buffoons", but also "Marlow, The User of Comedy".

As recent criticism has demonstrated,[16] Marlow is more than a narrator or moral judge, and he is a man who notes the comic in situations which are not essentially comic in terms of what appears to be their theme, at least to him, and he is a man whose role of narrator is merely part of his role as character and is that which, as such, can be considered a reflection of the changes and conflicts in his being and self as the novels in which he appears proceed. By this I mean that a careful study of Marlow's narrative manner will reveal much about him as a character caught up in the many tensions and ambiguities of an action and an identification with another character. In other words, his narrative art is not simply a way of getting a story told. If Marlow then is to be considered as the user (and creator) as well as the noter of the comic, or low comic, then this comic dimension or element in Conrad would in some cases be considered as part of a subjective reality or the reality of only one character. And Marlow is many things and has a good deal of elusiveness. Basically, he is a man seeking and dis-

---

ment of human events", and laughter is initiated by the transformation of a person into a thing. A major process of comedy is repetition, a parallel to mechanisation. Comedy fixes our attention on the realm of gesture and works with puppetlike movements.

[16] Especially W. Y. Tindall in his "Apology For Marlow", in *From Jane Austen to Joseph Conrad*, eds., R. C. Rathburn and M. Steinmann, Jr. (Minneapolis, 1958), pp. 274-285.

covering, bearing great weights and reflecting great tensions, learning what it perhaps means to be. And as he struggles with this knowledge, and becomes caught in the multiple complexities and contradictions and paradoxes which are seen as part of this knowledge, he reacts, and suffers in perplexity. Thus, any examination of this problem of what is called farce or burlesque in Conrad would have either to begin or to conclude with Marlow. In any case, he cannot be ignored, and one must seek the clues to his particular nature to explain this comic element, and also understand that this comic element is one of the major clues to his particular nature.

One reads Conrad's darker works like *Heart of Darkness* and *Lord Jim*, and less dark works like *Victory*, and finds something to be found in such works as *Youth* and *Falk*, works possibly having serious themes, but themes which are hardly treated seriously. As Jim and Marlow struggle to define being and to know themselves, as Marlow wanders in various nightmares, and as Heyst fights the great struggle of his life; as these things happen, ship's officers in orange-striped pajamas, men in flight from legions of centipedes, cats who hit apes and then lecture them on ingratitude, men who rush about and try to extinguish fires with little tin pails with holes in their bottoms all prance about. What they are doing in these dark and serious contexts is a question. Why is Martin Ricardo not just a cat, but every member of the cat family; why is Jim's abandonment of the *Patna* to be put into juxtaposition with the movements of the ship's four officers as they struggle to get a life-boat free and as they threaten and bark in the life-boat after the jump? And why in a story about the elemental and primitive in men, about cannibalism and self-preservation, as in *Falk*, is there a drunken character who tosses a banana?

II

THE HOLE IN THE BOTTOM OF THE PAIL: COMEDY AND THEME IN *HEART OF DARKNESS**

1

At the center of *Heart of Darkness*, at a stage of a dark and sombre journey, and not always perceived on a first reading, is a bit of low comedy marked by a stout man with black moustaches who tears up and down paths during a strange fire and who goes to the rescue with a small tin pail containing a hole in its bottom. This scene of the fire at the central station, which is a scene defined by burning calico, the beating of a native, and the pilgrim with his one phrase that everyone is behaving "splendidly", does not exist in isolation. During this scene:

> One evening a grass shed full of calico, cotton prints, beads, and I don't know what else burst into a blaze so suddenly that you would have thought the earth had opened to let an avenging fire consume all that trash. I was smoking my pipe quietly by my dismantled steamer, and saw them all cutting capers in the light, with their arms lifted high, when the stout man with moustaches came tearing down to the river, a tin pail in his hand, assured me that everybody was "behaving splendidly, splendidly", dipped about a quart of water and tore back again. I noticed there was a hole in the bottom of his pail.[1]

Marlow has observed men "cutting capers", a man who comes tearing up and down paths, and a hole in a pail. The point is that there is a considerable amount of "cutting capers" and rushing about with pails with holes in their bottoms in *Heart of Darkness*.

* This chapter appeared in shorter form in *Studies in Short Fiction*, II (1965), 113-123.
[1] *Conrad's Heart of Darkness and the Critics*, ed. Bruce Harkness (San Francisco, 1960), p. 19. All future references to *Heart of Darkness* will be to this edition.

2

Restraint and the lack of it, as used in relationship to various characters and actions, is an important term in the novel, and as such seems not only a yardstick for judgment, but also a direction for salvation,[2] at least on some level, although it should be noted that because the manager of the central station and the accountant of the outer station have their respective restraints,[3] and because they are who they are, it might be obvious that restraint, without qualification, cannot be enough, for an agent is dying in the cabin of the accountant, and the manager has his conversations with his uncle. Nevertheless, Marlow tells us that he has his restraint, which is the thing which maintains and saves him, and this restraint is his attention to his work, an attention to surface truths, and a surface reality. Yet, despite what he says, he still has or finds much time to observe his surroundings and to give a kind of chronicle of the damned, or something he can, himself, relate to the circle of some Inferno,[4] or in one place to a grove of death, a place reflecting all the various attitudes of pain and despair, apathy, wretchedness, and hopelessness. Now *Heart of Darkness* is many things, but there seems to be considerable agreement that it is primarily a journey toward some kind of self hood, and possibly an encounter with a second self, or with the Freudian *id* or the Jungian shadow.[5] Marlow makes the journey, drawn on as a silly bird before a hypnotic snake, his image, telling us much about the nature and progress of his journey; and he tells us:

[2] See the essay by Harold Collins, "Kurtz, the Cannibals, and the Second Rate Helmsman", *Western Humanities Review*, VIII (1954), 299-310. See also *Heart of Darkness*, p. 51, p. 45, p. 36.
[3] Marlow says of the manager, "He was just the kind of man who would wish to preserve appearances. That was his restraint. "*Heart of Darkness*, p. 37.
[4] "... it seemed to me I had stepped into the gloomy circle of some Inferno". *Heart of Darkness*, p. 13.
[5] See Guerard, *Conrad the Novelist*, p. 39. Moser in his *Joseph Conrad: Achievement and Decline*, p. 80, sees the journey in the less specific terms of a journey which is like travelling into one's past, and into the world of one's dreams, and the subconscious. Thrale, in his "Marlow's Quest", *UTQ*, XXIV (1955), 351-8, sees Marlow confronting what it means to be human in his confrontation of Kurtz.

It was the farthest point of navigation and the culminating point of my experience. It seemed somehow to throw a kind of light on everything about me — and into my thoughts. It was sombre enough too — and pitiful — not extraordinary in any way — not very clear either.[6]

Marlow is discovering about himself — in his recounting, reliving the journey and his discovery — and he, in doing this, seems always to be in danger of losing himself, of falling, of not understanding, and of not being able to see. One recalls his return from the inner station, the sparsity of its details, the abruptness of its narration, and his nearly fatal illness, which is described in terms of a spiritual condition suggesting what the earlier grove of death suggests, a malady defined as a "passage through some inconceivable world that had no hope in it and no desire".[7] And "no hope" and "no desire" should be emphasized. For possibly, at this point, Marlow has entered the grove of death which he saw and imaged earlier, with its attitudes of despair and abandonment.[8] In any case, Marlow will seem to want to know, and he will, as a result, be in danger of knowing too much for him to bear, and he will seem to maintain control, to order with conscious discipline, to remain sane, to know clearly what the journey involves. The world he enters is called by him a nightmare world,[9] and there seems to be a first-occuring choice for him which is the choice between reality and attention to objective matters and a world where things happen with neither logic nor meaning. Yet, when Kurtz is finally encountered, there remains only a second-occuring choice which is called a "choice of nightmares", and here, where this second choice only exists, one strives to find some kind of controlling feature — such as an adequate symbol for Kurtz — and the answer to the question — What is the significance of Marlow's change in terms from one choice to another choice in relationship to his illness, and, of course, to that which follows his illness, his visit to

---

[6] *Heart of Darkness*, p. 5.

[7] *Ibid.*, pp. 62-3.

[8] *Ibid.*, p. 13. "Black shapes crouched, lay, sat between the trees, leaning against the trunks, clinging to the earth, half effaced within the dim light, in all the attitudes of pain, abandonment, and despair."

[9] *Ibid.*, p. 11. "It was like a weary pilgrimage amongst hints for nightmares."

the Intended, where she is, as William York Tindall has noted,[10] both darkness and light, where she is saint and sister to savage? Nevertheless, Marlow must endeavor to maintain himself, and he tells us that, "I had to watch the steering and circumvent those snags, and get the tin-pot along by hook or by crook. There was surface-truth enough in these things to save a wiser man."[11] Yet, Marlow, as I have said, watches other things; he has time enough to watch the pilgrims "cutting capers" and to observe the hole in the bottom of the pail. And at the beginning of his journey, as he approaches his first destination and hears the strange dream-like names, he calls our attention to the suggestion of "some sordid farce acted in front of a sinister back-cloth",[12] and, as he observes the French gunboat shelling the bush, he further remarks: "There was a touch of insanity in the proceeding, a sense of lugubrious drollery in the sight."[13] "Sordid farce", "lugubrious drollery", "insanity": these are the definers of the now beginning nightmare, and a suggestion of something else — a clue to a direction to be taken, a hope of salvation, and Marlow's subtle purpose.

3

Comedy, of a certain type, is probably the best entrance into the *Heart of Darkness* — at least, it seems to be Marlow's mode of entrance here. A landscape which suggests a medieval hell marked by chilly ravines, stony hills, paths everywhere, a glaring sun, and solitude seems composed of not only the grotesque and the night-marish, but also that which seems related here to this grotesque and nightmarish — a sort of low comedy, and a series of gestures and situations and incongruities which would seem to add up to something slightly more than a fantastic dream. Marlow perceives that what he calls a "flabby devil" is running the show — which he has labelled a farce — and he makes this "flabby devil" a bit of a buffoon. Everything here, every step of the journey, at least to the central station, if not past it, is marked by the comic, and the type

---

[10] In his essay, "Apology for Marlow", pp. 280-81.
[11] *Heart of Darkness*, p. 31.
[12] *Ibid.*, p. 10.
[13] *Ibid.*, p. 11.

of comic best called low comedy or farce, for it is further defined by pace, which is very quick — in keeping with what is structured as a dream-journey — and defined by intensity, as in the case of scenes marked by violence, where people rush back and forth and where characters come tearing up and down paths, when they are not dancing, arms lifted high, and stop for a minute to make explanations and assurances. And in the hole at the bottom of a pail coupled with a burning of trash and a man rushing to put out this burning, there is an essential futility and purposelessness, which is a source of comedy, and which is in violent contrast to the frantic assumptions of purpose characterizing the actions of this man who rushes down a path. I suppose we would at least smile if a man in checkered pants and long sword, and possibly with a long red nose, were to go wholeheartedly into some activity with a great deal of formality and procedure, to conduct an experiment, or boil an egg.

The world that Marlow observes is characterized by him as a "merry dance of death".[14] In some old woodcuts — those of Holbein, for instance — the dance of death, which was a dance of skeletons and dukes and princes and popes, had its comic aspects, and naturally a great potential for comedy, in its contrasts and reductive qualities. Skeletons and Death dance a good deal in *Heart of Darkness*; each sin and folly — greed, lust ambition, and their effects — is rendered through concrete images suggesting an insane jesting, a lunatic jollity. Marlow is quick to observe this, and he sees much in these terms, or chooses to see much in these terms, seeking always every intimation of the absurd. He finds that everywhere.

A French gunboat is shelling the shore:

Pop, would go one of the six-inch guns; a small flame would dart and vanish, a little white smoke would disappear, a tiny projectile would give a feeble screech — and nothing happened.[15]

A railroad is being built:

---

[14]   *Ibid.*, p. 11. "We called at some more places with farcical names, where the merry dance of death and trade goes on in a still and earthly atmosphere as of an overheated catacomb."
[15]   *Ibid.*, p. 11.

A horn tooted to the right, and I saw the black people run. A heavy and dull detonation shook the ground, a puff of smoke came out of the cliff, and that was all. No change appeared on the face of the rock.[16]

And, as he proceeds:

I avoided a vast artificial hole somebody had been digging on the slope, the purpose of which I found it impossible to divine. It wasn't a quarry or a sandpit anyhow. It was just a hole.[17]

And he saw:

Once a white man in an unbuttoned uniform, camping on the path with an armed escort of lank Zanzibaris, very hospitable and festive — not to say drunk. Was looking after the upkeep of the road, he declared. Can't say I saw any road or any upkeep, unless the body of a middle-aged Negro, with a bullet-hole in the forehead, upon which I absolutely stumbled three miles farther on, may be considered as a permanent improvement.[18]

Furthermore, there are the absurdities of Marlow's fat and fleshly companion, continually fainting, found upset in the bush, litter and all, who has come out to make money, "of course"; of the chief accountant, who, having come out to "get a breath of fresh air", appears in high-starched collar, white cuffs, a light alpaca jacket, snowy throusers, clean neck-tie, varnished boots, and with a penholder behind his ear; of the members of the El Dorado group; of a pilgrim in pink pajamas: and of a papier-maché Mephistopheles, with his one candle. These men and caricatures backbite and gossip as if they were seated in various boulevard cafes, and there were no dying man in a cabin, no Kurtz, no darkness — and they plot and speak of futures and careers, saying that one will go far in an obviously futureless land, where there is only a primal timelessness. The culminating vision of all this farce and slapstick is what occurs at the central station, a place where a group of pilgrims sit up nights waiting to take pot-shots at a probably indifferent hippo, and where an excitable chap with pail and moustaches will assure

---

[16]   *Ibid.*, p. 12.
[17]   *Ibid.*, p. 13.
[18]   *Ibid.*, p. 16.

Marlow that everybody is behaving "splendidly". *And indeed they are.*[19]

4

Since it exists in the context of a journey and the total action of this journey, this comedy — its sources and incidents — strangely placed in the sombre discourse of this novel, is to be viewed in the light of certain aspects of style and structure here in order to determine and to clarify its function. When F. R. Leavis, in his *The Great Tradition*,[20] began his attack on the novel by stating that, while Conrad's art at its best was when Conrad's comment emerged from the thing rendered as part of the tone, there were, however, "places in *Heart of Darkness* where we become aware of comment as an interposition and worse, as an intrusion, at times an exasperating one", for (Leavis continues), "hadn't he, we find ourselves asking, overworked 'inscrutable', 'inconceivable', 'unspeakable', and that kind of word already?" — an "adjectival insistence", an insistence which urges upon the reader and auditor an inexpressive and incomprehensible mystery; when he made these criticisms he was overlooking, it is now usual to say, that it is Marlow who is creating the story, who is more than narrator, and who, as another critic notes, "reiterates often enough that he is recounting a spiritual voyage of self discovery".[21] Nevertheless, Leavis' criticism may direct us to a disturbing element in the novel. I think I under-

---

[19] In brief, the sources and incidents of comedy in *Heart of Darkness* are, then, the playing of the illusion of purpose against an obvious and stronger purposelessness and aimlessness and an incongruity where there is a little tin pail to put out a fire, where there is a character dressed in a certain way, or there is someone to speak of Kurtz's going far and getting ahead, as if he were discussing the matter anywhere but where he is, or there is an accountant teaching a native to starch collars in an environment where collars are of no real significance. There is also the sordid bucaneer talk and braggadocio of the members of the El Dorado group, and, of course, the name — El Dorado — itself. Furthermore, rigidity, the mechanical, involving repeated movements, coupled with frantic motions, serves as a source of this comedy. The pilgrims cut "capers" during a fire, wander about with staves, and one tears up and down paths.

[20] p. 177.

[21] Guerard, *Conrad the Novelist*, p. 38.

stand what Leavis means — *Heart of Darkness* has two styles, which is to say that Marlow has two styles. The first involves what Marvin Mudrick[22] has called the double-plot, where the journey is "finely coincident" with its network of details — its moral nature revealing itself in details and facts, for a developing order of actions is symbolic of a developing state of the spirit. The material actions in themselves have independent reality, yet they are analogous to some inner or spiritual reality. But, Mudrick continues, *this often breaks down*, and Conradian rhetoric is employed in place of details, with an "oracular-ruminative" style replacing a narrative-descriptive one.

Yet, the structure of *Heart of Darkness* seems clear. The novel follows a circular form, beginning and ending with a frame, using a journey which moves forward and then back. The journey itself involves an outer station, a central station, and an inner station, all having spiritual and probable psychological equivalents. One proceeds inward, and within a heart of darkness lies a deeper heart, the core within the core, and the night when Marlow goes out into the jungle after Kurtz, and the moment of his shock and "discovery".

The stages of this journey are connected by the river, certain controlling images such as the serpent image, or what is done with light and dark images, a movement in a certain direction, and towards a certain destination coupled with an urgency to get there, but most of all by the narrative telling of this journey. The latter has a forcefulness and impetus, and moves almost relentlessly forward, and, since this is a dream or the suggestion of a nightmare, no logical connections are developed, except for the logic of the movement itself. But the narrative is also controlled, almost tightly so; and the narrator-artist-arranger not only chooses meaningful details, but illuminates them through a controlling device that Conrad has shown Marlow using elsewhere. If there is any danger in the minor devils of the outer and central stations — and reference should be made here to the number of critics who see various underworld associations in this work, and who see Virgilian and Dantean

---

[22]   See his "The Originality of Conrad," *Hudson Review*, XI (1958), 546-9.

parallels,[23] and reference should also be made here to the terms used by Marlow to describe his nearly fatal illness, terms which might imply that these devils or fallen men are dangers — one does not really feel this danger, for Marlow is able to keep not only his sanity, but also the clarity of a guide that might be called a "moral guide". In other words, he could be a man who knows what something is, and who can understand and see. But only in a limited sense does Marlow's devotion to surface reality and his concentration on real things such as the surf, the native rowers, and his wrecked steamer save him and allow him to see, or not to see — more than this, and quite important, Marlow is a civilized man[24] and has what appears to be an understanding which is articulated through a manner of telling about what he has seen. He can see and can discover the proper defining correlative for what he is encountering. In other words, Marlow encounters the pilgrims and minor devils and fallen men of his journey, and the hints for a nightmare, and immediately makes associations, creating images which allow him to control what he has seen, as well as to control what he perceives to be a nightmare.

It is Marlow who, as I have said, introduced the sense of farce, the touch of insanity, the marks of "lugubrious drollery". The names of the native coastal ports sound absurd and farcical, and hence he is given his controlling image. Low comedy in a certain context has certain associations, and separate from its function in relationship to the teller, it can serve as an adequate correlative for some kind of evil, defining its quality and essence, for all the follies of *Heart of Darkness*' pilgrims have a thing in common, in that they suggest disorder and lack of control, which is to say they belong with the inhuman or subhuman. The latter can be seen when Marlow refers to the "short flipper" of the manager's uncle when

[23]   Lilian Feder, for instance, in her "Marlow's Descent into Hell", *NCF*, IX (1955), 280-92. And R. O. Evans in "Conrad's Underworld", *MFS*, II (1956), 56-62.

[24]   Marlow, as contrasted with the other characters of the novel, represents, I think, the best of European civilization. And as representative of this civilization, he best embodies its modes of perception, protection, and consciousness. His use of irony, for instance, is an aspect of this. Also he has a certain humanity lacking elsewhere.

he overhears the conversation between this uncle and the manager concerning Kurtz.[25] Marlow, in a sense, is dehumanizing verbally this man by seeing him in terms of the bestial and something less than human. Low comedy, involving absurd costumes, false gestures, frantic and aimless movements, and the suggestion of knockabout clowning, shows the lack of control and disorder in that which is being encountered, and the seeming abundance of control and order on the part of the one who is doing the encountering, and the imaging.

Marlow controls his material through images of farce and a concommitant irony. Each experience and detail, as the journey progresses, has its absurd element, and all this as Marlow looks after and towards real things or so he says. But Marlow is really observing carefully what he sees, and it seems nonsense to say that he is putting all his faith in and attention upon surface reality, for he is too sensitive for this, and he *does not have that much control.* And why — that is, if he could only pay attention to surface truths — would he be making the journey anyway? As he observes, he images and presents and draws the proper analogy, emphasizing the right detail, and keeping the nightmare, which is first seen from the outside, distant. The choice is still one between nightmare and no nightmare. Low comedy is also a means of keeping distance, and of avoiding attachment and involvement. There is clarity during and in the first stages of the journey, for Marlow knows what he sees, and he, in his defensive strategy, can also create or find the proper definers which suggest the spiritual implication of the pilgrim's folly, He seems to know who and what they are — aspects of an Inferno and vices, almost medieval in force — and their being is to be seen in the light of the farce, which is the difference between them and the telling of them. By this, I mean they are comic, but also that it is the comic element, and no other, that Marlow chooses to remember. Slapstick is the major definer, for while the fire at the central station, which is mysterious and seemingly meaningless, is defined in terms of that which is being burnt and the beating of a native, signifying greed and cruelty, if

[25] *Heart of Darkness*, p. 28.

not also apathy of a sort; there is more than this here, and the fire is defined in terms of the men with staves, the stout man with moustaches, and the noted pail. A French gunboat shoots puffs of smoke, and El Dorado Expedition appears and disappears, and a fat man speaks of money. The accountant may be admired because he has control, but he is still absurd and a representation of folly, of an evil, for he is indifferent and a man dies in his office, a detail which condemns him, as his incongruity and motley judge him, and explain him. Collars and pen-holders are as out of place here as ambition and its envy. In fact, nothing seems in place here — this is a landscape of ruin, with overturned cars and explosions, and nothing much happening.

When Leavis and Mudrick speak of two styles and a change of styles at the heart of this novel, and, I think, in the heart of Marlow; they might have been following the progress of a manner of relating incidents, and the progress of a low comedy. The comic image I speak of is a major aspect of the change they speak of, and, except for a very few places, such as in the case of the pilgrim in the pink pajamas, is missing from the novel's latter sections.[26] Of course, the obvious implication is that Kurtz is not and cannot be an object of farce, that he is to be seen as something or someone who is flexible, a person in flux, reaching the limits and boundaries of being, not rigidly defined and contained. If anything, in other words, he is an object for serious consideration, and his disorder is on another plane, not graspable by means of metaphor or simple image. This is at least how Marlow might feel, but, nevertheless, the control implicit in Marlow through his use of a certain type of manner of telling appears to be lacking or weakened on some other levels, suggesting that more than a question of how we are to view Kurtz, as opposed to how we are to view the pilgrims, is involved. The earlier style of *Heart of Darkness* contains what is called farce, a heavy sense of insane absurdity, but also clear images and stated

---

[26]   It is true that Kurtz's Russian admirer is dressed in the costume of a harlequin, but this is to have him primarily illustrate one aspect of the encounter — that fools (or the innocent) cannot be touched. See *Heart of Darkness*, p. 43. "Of course, you may be too much of a fool to go wrong — too dull even to know you are being assaulted by the powers of darkness."

judgments, and very important, a clear and smooth narrative movement, centered upon a progression of details and incidents. But as Marlow approaches the inner station, he becomes more a voice and less a master of ceremonies; and in two important places we can discover a stopping of the narrative movement and an inter-position of interpretation and explanation — where Marlow first begins to tell of his actual and direct and physical encountering of Kurtz, and the place where Marlow goes out into the jungle to seek Kurtz, a place best referred to as a "core within a core", because it is where he receives his moral shock and "discovery". In this latter place,[27] Marlow begins by relating what was happening — he comes upon Kurtz, etc. — "and then he interrupts this relation of events to speak of Kurtz's gratified and monstrous passions", his "mad" and "unlawful" soul. The narrative is only resumed with "I kept my head pretty well; but when I had him at last stretched on the couch, I wiped my forehead, while my legs shook under me as though I had carried half a ton on my back down that hill." This is a strange hiatus — although one might say that in the terror and sweat of his moral recognition, it was natural that all should be part of a daze, that he should not know (or care to tell) how he got him back. *And this is, it would seem, just the point.*

5

This daze which gives the apparent lie to Marlow's statement that he kept his head "pretty well", and which seems to indicate a change in him, a change seen in terms of Leavis' style shifts, Mudrick's movement from a narrative-descriptive mode to an "oracular-ruminative" one, in terms of an absence of controlling art, farce and comic definition in the novel's later sections, and in terms of what seems to be a breakdown in narrative movement, is evident most significantly in those parts of the novel which deal with what appears to be the aftermath or coda to Marlow's experi-ence. There is very much in the scene with the Intended suggesting that these breakdowns and changes might be considered intentional

[27]   *Heart of Darkness*, pp. 58-9.

and a major source of the novel's meaning. In a sense, this scene with the Intended illuminates, as well as symbolizes, all the movements in the novel we have been encountering, and it is central to any concern with the comic dimension of this journey in terms of its implications of control, both narrative and psychological.

This scene with the Intended, the one episode we are given after Marlow's sickness, illustrates some of the confusion and the failure of understanding or its repression that are suggested by the changes in style and narrative manner at the core of the novel. Tindall has spoken of a confusion of light and dark; "an irony of which Marlow is only half aware is the terrible confusion of light and dark that he reveals within himself. Darkness in white fog seems a fitting symbol."[28] This is shown in the episode with the Intended; Marlow, an apostle of light, enters the house of the woman who loved Kurtz and who mistook darkness for light; as he enters, darkness enters with him, growing deeper as he talks. He tries to preserve the light of the woman; yet, implied in her black dress and other accoutrements is that she really is not light. Along with this noted confusion of imagery, one can find on Marlow's part a confusion of judgments, amplifying and explaining the various exhaustions which became his after his encounter with Kurtz. The Intended is identified with the pure, with the unearthly glow shining in a darkness. But the darkness is triumphant, and she becomes a "tragic and familiar shade", resembling the savage woman in gesture and in stance. She is pure, yet horrible — a place of cruel and absurd mysteries.

The Intended is identified with light, the saving illusion, and faith. Her unearthly glow makes her one of those who could not be touched because they are apart from and above the things of the world. Yet, the darkness comes as she responds, an increasing darkness, and her sorrow in one moment becomes bound to Kurtz's death. Voices mingle. Marlow begins to feel terror. Having responded with a daze-like paralysis, followed by dull anger, infinite pity, fear and fright; his act — sometimes viewed as a moral act — of telling the lie is imaged as an act of control involving

[28]   "Apology For Marlow", pp. 280-1.

a pulling of oneself together. But if the Intended were pure, she could not be touched, for she could have no darkness within her — yet, Marlow feels that she does have darkness within her; he feels but does not know. The confrontation with "purity" perhaps involves as much a sweat and "moral shock" as does the confrontation with Kurtz and horror; the attempt to pull himself together is the lie, and her response is a cry which completely links her with the darkness and creates Marlow's final terror.

This is to suggest that not only do we have a confusion of light and dark in this scene, but also we have a confusion in the application of the images of light and dark, a confusion which is closely related to a confusion of judgment. Although Marlow as "moral guide" does not seem to know at this point, his voice is not silent. He passes contradictory judgments on the Intended — his responses and his terror, his mode of imagery, and his method of imaging give the lie to his ecstasy before something supposedly better. If there is any illumination at all, it is not Marlow's. Rather, it is the reader's — and it is that clear judgments are no longer possible. A voice also spoke of Kurtz and his unlawful passions. And Marlow became sick, lost his control, and his illness was described in symbolic terms, clearly related to the opening states and conditions of his journey and the hell he encounters, the grove of death. Apathy, hopelessness, despair, and abandonment are spiritual damnations; the grove of death is the striking symbol; and when Marlow lies near death, he is in a state without hope and without desire; for surrounded by a greyness and a sordid atmosphere of decay, he rots in his own grove of death. Yet, this is passed over quickly by Marlow, and in a way suggestive of the manner in which he halted and checked his narrative of his encounter with Kurtz on the dark night in the jungle. At the center of the novel's center there was hiatus. And this hiatus is part of the confusion and exhaustion which come to Marlow; that the scene with the Intended follows his sickness is important, for it represents the final and most intense representation of exactly the thing he has lost — *his controlling art*. Marlow is damned because he can no longer see, and yet he speaks and responds. His voice goes in one direction; his perception in another; and the Intended is pure but corrupt, innocent but fallen, unearthly but earthly, light but dark.

The final image of the narrator of the novel's frame is that of an English waterway leading into the heart of darkness. A recognition of this darkness which is essential to the novel, this comes mostly through Marlow, who carries darkness with and within him. The concluding paragraphs of the novel are possibly used to further illustrate the implications of this darkness — it spreads from person to person, from person to city to world. The narrator of the frame has perceived Marlow perceiving Kurtz. He is much like the reader in this respect. His image follows the narration of the scene with the Intended, and is the realization of the darkness in Marlow, the realization that he will carry his experience with him, forever.

In a letter of May 31, 1902, to William Blackwood, Conrad spoke of the final episode of *Heart of Darkness*, its last pages, "where the interview of the man and the girl locks in — as it were — the whole 30,000 words of narrative description into one suggestive view of a whole phase of life, and makes of that story something quite on another plane than an anecdote of a man who went mad in the centre of Africa".[29] As noted, there are confusions and darknesses in this scene with the Intended which amplify the falls and problems and confusions of the rest of the novel, and which parallel them; but not noted is that this scene has a complex movement which closely parallels the movement of the entire journey to the inner station. There is even a center here, with its equivalent "moral shock", and with reactions of a Marlow who does not really know. In a few pages, Conrad has included some of the major progressions and motifs of his entire novel.

Marlow goes, ostensibly, to give up the memory of Kurtz (he does not, for he tells and re-lives the journey), but, in reality, he has no clear perception of what it is that he wants. He speaks of an impulse of unconscious loyalty, but also of the "fulfillment of one of those ironic necessities that lurk in the facts of human existence". But he does not know. The city is imaged as it had been imaged at the beginning of the first and major journey; Marlow

[29]   *Letters to William Blackwood and David S. Meldrum*, ed. William Blackburn (Durham, N.C., 1958), p. 154.

begins in a "well-kept alley in a cemetery", in the white sepulchre, the dead city, which had been imaged as an entrance to hell. The vision is one of Kurtz and darkness; part of the vision seems to enter the house with Marlow, as if Marlow himself were bringing this darkness into the house.

The Intended strikes Marlow as beautiful — a delicate shade of truthfulness, without mental reservation, without suspicion or a thought for herself. Light remains on her forehead; her dark eyes present a guileless, profound, confident and trustful glance.

Yet, darkness enters the room and Marlow feels it to be his duty to keep back the invading darkness for the salvation of another soul. In this room which is tomb-like and deceptive, he begins to fear and to feel terror. Her look of awful desolation links her sorrow and Kurtz's death, and Marlow wonders what he is doing there in a place he refers to as a "place of cruel and absurd mysteries":

I asked myself what I was doing there, with a sensation of panic in my heart as though I had blundered into a place of cruel and absurd mysteries not fit for a human being to behold.[30]

Marlow speaks of bowing before her faith and her saving illusion — he speaks of her unearthly glow in the darkness, identifying her with those who cannot be touched — "Or you may be such a thunderingly exalted creature as to be altogether deaf and blind to anything but heavenly sights and sounds"[31] — yet, this darkness is triumphant and something from which Marlow can neither defend her nor himself. As they speak, Marlow makes associations and invokes further darkness; he hears voices combined and he begins to sweat, to have his "shock". Her unextinguishable light of love and belief carries him into an appalled dumbness, and there is despair in his heart.

Marlow seems almost paralyzed, or, as is proper in a novel where enchantment and a snake image are of importance, suggesting a major theme of enchantment, hypnotized; he speaks

---

[30]   *Heart of Darkness*, p. 67.
[31]   *Ibid.*, p. 43.

more and more in a daze or a trance, as he makes associations and hears voices:

"And of all this", she went on mournfully, "of all his promise, and of all his greatness, of his generous mind, of his noble heart, nothing remains — nothing but a memory. You and I —."
  "*We shall always remember him*", I said hastily.
  "No!" she cried. "It is impossible that all this should be lost — that such a life should be sacrificed to leave nothing — but sorrow. You know what vast plans he had. I knew of them too — I could not perhaps understand — but others knew of them. Something must remain. His words, at least, have not died."
  "*His words will remain*", I said.
  "And his example", she whispered to herself. "Men looked up to him — his goodness shown in every act. His example —." "True", I said: "*his example too. Yes, his example. I forgot that.*"[32] (Italics mine).

Identifying through gesture the Intended with the savage girl, he calls her a "tragic and familiar shade", and he goes through a succession of emotions involving dull anger, infinite pity, his mumbling, his muffled voice and the chill gripping on his chest, his fright and terror. It is only through the lie that this ceases — the lie is imaged as an act of pulling himself together — yet, it is followed by his heart standing still, stopping dead, at the hearing of her "exulting and terrible cry". At this point it seems the house would collapse, and it would have been too dark to do otherwise, to tell her, to render justice to Mr. Kurtz, as Marlow terms it.

  The following things are then apparent in this final scene: a confusion of judgments, for Marlow makes her pure at the same time he images her as a shade; and an increasing fear and terror as she speaks and as Marlow's imagination makes the destroying kinship — her voice, Kurtz's voice; her gesture, the gesture of the savage. The Intended is identified with light, but a light of death, the whiteness of the tomb and city, as well as a light of purity and faith; but she is also identified with a darkness, the darkness of her heart, of Marlow's perception and recognition, and of that which underlies the whiteness of the tomb and the city. She, like Kurtz, is a place of absurd and cruel mysteries, and also, like Kurtz, she

[32]   *Ibid.*, p. 68.

is a shade and a voice, a voice terrible yet mesmeric. Marlow's increasing reactions are like his reactions to Kurtz — daze, anger, pity, fear, and "moral shock". One could say that he seems to be reliving his journey again on the smaller scale of this vital analogue, which Conrad calls the episode which locks in the entire novel.

The lie itself is not the moral act that Wilcox believes it to be,[33] for it involves neither mercy nor purification — nor is the Intended spiritual and faithful — another critic, Dowden, is closer to the truth of the matter when he speaks of the Intended as a "dim, almost spectral figure".[34] Rather, the lie's importance rests in what is happening to Marlow, not in what will happen to the Intended, and this is the way that it is presented:

I pulled myself together and spoke slowly. "The last word he pronounced was your name."[35]

It is an act of control, an attempt to hold back the panic and the fright that are Marlow's as he encounters this mystery, the parallel to Kurtz's. But, as at the center of his journey to the inner station, he fails here, losing his control and becoming a voice, imaging one way, passing judgments another. There are peculiar reactions for an act supposedly an act of compassion and mercy. The Intended responds with an exulting and terrible cry — a savage cry — and Marlow's heart stops dead (his "moral shock"?) — she is clearly identified with Kurtz and the savage now, where, before, there was merely the chaos in Marlow's mind, reflected by his image making. The horror is that through this identification Marlow's lie has not really saved the Intended — if Marlow is to save her from the darkness — or rather it has saved her — from the perception of this darkness, but not from the darkness itself — *but has not saved Marlow.* And perhaps then there is no real distinction between the darkness and the perception of the darkness. Marlow acts as if there were and responds as if there were not.

[33] "Conrad's Complicated Presentations of Symbolic Imagery in *Heart of Darkness*", *PQ*, XXXIX (1960), 14.
[34] "The Light and the Dark: Imagery and Thematic Development in Conrad's Heart of Darkness", *Rice Institute Pamphlets*, XLIV (1957), 48.
[35] *Heart of Darkness*, p. 69.

And he flees in disorder. When he says the house would collapse, it is not only because of the lie, and its association with the kinship between Marlow and Kurtz and with mortality and Marlow's fall, but also because of a lie in the context of the Intended's unexpected but sensed response. The irony is that the lie which identifies Marlow with death and with Kurtz is used to save a woman also identified with Kurtz — and in a similar way — but has the effect of proving her kinship and of reaffirming his own relationship to Kurtz. I detect something like another choice of nightmares here.

Thus one should suggest that the final scene of *Heart of Darkness* is an analogue to the entire novel, for its action and direction and deceptions parallel those of the main action, which is the journey itself. It is the culmination of the journey and the direct link to the frame narrator's last words, but it is more than that — it is the journey repeated and re-recognized. In a dead city, it is another journey to another heart of darkness, a heart of darkness in a civilized setting. It contains a light which is really dark and the confusion of Marlow as he passes conflicting judgments. He stands without defenses, vulnerable, in an increasing numbness, reacting here as he had reacted to Kurtz there. His lie, not an act of redemption, not an act of mercy, is a moral shock of a sort again, for once again kinship is recognized, and with similar violence, through a savage cry which illuminates further an image. And it is a moral shock in another similar and significant way, for it relates to the inadequacies, deceptions, and limitations of his acts of control. Standing in terror, Marlow has a dull awareness of perception — his kinship to the darkness (his lie) and her kinship to the darkness (her response to the lie). Marlow carries the darkness with him, not only as an image, but as the ability to make images. If he is still the artist, he is the dark artist and the artist of the irrational and of uncontrolled fear. His visit to the Intended has at its center what the major journey itself had at its center — a voice revealing, obscuring, repressing. Significantly, it follows his sickness — which best implies his fall — in terms of the novel's structure and is to be seen as an amplification of this sickness and as an expression of all the other changes which have occurred in his being. His sickness carries with it the burden of non-comprehension and the recognition of kinship; its terms are the terms of a wearied civilization and of a sickened consciousness, its defenses gone, its power debilitated, existing in a state of sordid, grey apathy. The scene is the transition to the final remarks of the frame narrator — not only does it present the heart of darkness in civilization, extending and amplifying Conrad's theme as well as the presentation of Marlow and what the darkness really means, but it also is that which leads directly to the perception of the narrator. The white city is closer to London and us than the inner station is.

At the heart of Marlow's development, journey, and fall, a fall illuminated in this scene with the Intended and in the various changes of the journey, centered in a movement away from a comic image and irony, which is also a movement away from narrative art, from objective style, from controlling art and from a choice between reality and nightmare; at the heart of Marlow's moral and spiritual exhaustion is the identification made between him and Kurtz. If there is any cause here, it is to be sought in terms of the establishment of this identification and fact of kinship, the most important act of the journey and the novel, for it signifies the movement from one area of experience to another, and, of course, the sickness and terror to be.

Appeal to kinship, to complicity, to recognition — indicated especially through the importance of the various glances of the natives — is an important motif. Although it is resisted on the lesser demoniac level of the pilgrims through Marlow's controlling consciousness, the major kinship and recognition — that involving Marlow and Kurtz — is not resisted, but rather accepted, as a choice of nightmares — and even, in a sense, to be used as part of Marlow's battery of defenses employed to keep his distance from the hell he encounters at the outer and central stations, or what he thinks to be this hell. Marlow hears the name Kurtz on few occasions. From the accountant he learns: "He is a very remarkable person. ... was at present in charge of a trading post, a very important one, in the true ivory country, at 'the very bottom of there. Sends in as much ivory as all the others together. ...'"[36] At the

---

[36]   *Ibid.*, p. 15.

central station, Marlow is further told that Kurtz is sick, that he is exceptional, and that he is of greatest importance to the company; and from the brickmaker and manager's spy he learns that Kurtz is a prodigy, of the gang of virtue, who has special ideas. Marlow's reactions are, to say the least, hardly apparent. He is either silent or mildly curious, but in a most natural way. He is slightly impatient and can think, "Hang Kurtz"[37] but this is the result of frustration and a sunken steamboat. It is only when he encounters the brickmaker's insinuations that he takes his first positive action towards Kurtz, lying,[38] the importance of which is stressed by the identification of the lie with corruption and mortality and by its reappearance in the context of the scene with the Intended. The reasons given are veiled — merely the notion that the lie would be a help to Kurtz — but the action also seems to be an immediate response, suggesting motives and expected results which are not terribly clear. Marlow can be said to be choosing his allegiances — or rather, all one can really say is that, in some way, Marlow is making distinctions and establishing involvement, if not kinship. Possibly, he is even using Kurtz to protect himself against the brickmaker, but this will only be folly, as shown later.

The fourth time Kurtz is mentioned is in the context of the arrival of the El Dorado Exploring Expedition at the end of part one of the novel. But here, Marlow, however, affirms that Kurtz remains just a word for him, even though he has seen the sinister light of the painting; and he further affirms his lack of interest in Kurtz. He has become curious and every so often gives some thought to Kurtz, but this is a restrained curiosity, and a curiosity which is aroused only because it appears to Marlow that Kurtz had come equipped with moral ideas of some sort. Marlow tells us that he wonders whether Kurtz would climb to the top, and how he would set about his work once there.[39]

The scene which follows these remarks and which commences part two of the novel — the overheard conversation of the man-

[37]   *Ibid.*, pp. 18-9.
[38]   *Ibid.*, p. 21.
[39]   *Ibid.*, p. 26.

ager and his uncle — strangely enough suggests that the identification has been firmly made and that involvement has taken place.
"As for me, I seemed to see Kurtz for the first time. It was a
distinct glimpse: the dugout, four paddling savages, and the lone
white man turning his back suddenly on the headquarters, on
relief, on thoughts of home — perhaps; setting his face towards the
depths of the wilderness, towards his empty and desolate station. ...
Perhaps, he was just a fine fellow who stuck to his work for its
own sake".[40] Marlow overhears Kurtz's ideas, and the response of
the manager's uncle:

"And the pestiferous absurdity of his talk", continued the other; "he
bothered me enough when he was here. 'Each station should be like a
beacon on the road towards better things, a centre for trade of course,
but also for humanizing, improving, instructing.' Conceive you — that
ass! And he wants to be manager!"[41]

and his reaction is almost violent. This is clear from the image he
chooses at this point: "I was surprised to see how near they were —
right under me. I could have spat upon their hats." Kurtz is seen
as a man facing the wilderness, as a man who works, as a man with
ideas, who is called an ass by the cynical and backbiting devils of the
central station, and Marlow measures distance by spittle. The
choice of figure is perhaps the result of identification, for one can
consider all the possibilities of figures of speech in this situation,
and this specific figure of speech. To say one "could have spat
upon their hats" expresses not only an idea of closeness, but also
an idea of feeling and judgment — the reaction follows the calling
of Kurtz an ass, and the violence in the act of spitting is the violence
of Marlow's emotional response at this point.

Thus at the beginning of the second part of this novel the fact
that the identification, or kinship, has been established is suggested
by the violence of a reaction presented through a figure of speech
which clearly renders attitude. That this should follow the speaker's
condemnation of Kurtz's "ideas" is fully significant. And after
this Marlow's response to Kurtz is marked by an urgency to get to

[40] *Ibid.*, p. 27.
[41] *Ibid.*, p. 28.

him, to meet him, and a despair at the possibility that he might not be able to. But the problem is still how this identification between Kurtz and Marlow is established, for it is an identification which leads to the core of the novel, the "moral shock", the sickness, the scene with the Intended. One has seen the five stages or steps of this development, but what has been revealed? There are only five steps, and *no clear*, *logical progression* — silence is interrupted by two positive actions — the lie and the expression of an image. The movement is unclear — the steps are merely silence, more silence, the lie, modified and qualified curiosity, violent reaction and urgency to reach Kurtz. One is given no in-between steps; the kinship is merely suggested, and it is with some shock that one sees that it is firmly established — particularly in Marlow's urgency to reach Kurtz — without quite knowing how or why.

Marlow apparently knows enough about Kurtz to make the identification, or to allow it to be made. He knows about the ivory, the painting, the idealism, the loneliness, and the facing of the solitude. Moreover, he is in constant contact with the backbiting and attitudes of the pilgrims, and he, of course, reacts to this. But nothing else. And which of these elements really is the basis of the attraction? One might say several things — before Marlow's violent reaction, there is given the image of the man alone, and this is followed by a repeating of Kurtz's ideas about each station, and the attitude and response of the pilgrims. But the lie occurs earlier, and by this time it may be assumed that commitment and involvement have already taken place, at least unconsciously, or not with full consciousness. The contrast of Kurtz with the pilgrims, something which seems to set him apart, the suggestion of some kind of strength: these things obviously urge the identification on. And if the identification is further urged on by the image of the man alone, the image which most strongly precedes the urgency and compulsion to reach Kurtz and which seems to provide the transition from the basic indifference of Marlow's response at the end of part one to the violence and anxiety of his response at the beginning of part two, then it might seem that an image basically sentimental exists in the context of implications of moral choice. The sympathy for the man alone raises serious questions. But what is the first step? — a kind of medieval sin of curiosity,[42] coupled with these other things, or something else? All that is given are hints, and Marlow himself never speaks of causes or reasons here; it just happens, and this must be perceived, for one is not told. Possibly, the reasons lie in all these things and all the information that Marlow gains about Kurtz and the pilgrims, but, as presented, it remains mysterious and perhaps incomprehensible.

As the controlling images of the journey of *Heart of Darkness* are the nightmare and the insane dream as well as the hypnotic snake ("But there was in it one river especially, a mighty big river, that you could see on the map resembling an immense snake uncoiled ... it fascinated me as a snake would a bird — a silly little bird"),[43] it is in this manner that the identification between Marlow and Kurtz is made. Marlow wakes up one day to find the kinship clearly there. There are no causal relationships and connections — the dream has its own logic. How this kinship got to be there is hidden and represents most likely the operation of the unconscious, suggesting that this thing must be inevitable, that this thing is beyond will or control. This is not to say that Marlow does not realize the sordid aspects of Kurtz, for, later on, as he proceeds toward the inner station, he speaks of this "approach to this Kurtz grubbing for ivory in the wretched bush", which was "beset by as many dangers as though he had been an enchanted princess sleeping in a fabulous castle".[44] Kurtz is both an ivory grubber and an enchanted princess. This is the analogue, the important symbol, for the entire relationship, for the establishment of kinship and identification, for this identification involves both *enchantment* and abhorrence. One might even go beyond suggesting enchantment as an explanation or a symbol for what is happening, and one might suggest that it is a major part of theme itself. The dream moves on relentlessly as the subject stands to the side, abhorring, yet fascinated. Marlow perceives — this analogue and image is built upon all he has been given and expresses the two-sided and

---

[42] This would be in keeping with the medieval atmosphere of this work — its allegorical landscapes and its morality types. But this is only a suggestion.
[43] *Heart of Darkness*, p. 5.
[44] *Ibid.*, p. 37.

dual aspects of this kinship — the ivory, the hostility, the idealism, and the loneliness.

What is remarkable here is that in a section of the novel which is marked and defined by Marlow's control and organizing defenses, a section which enables him to remain relatively calm and to keep detachment and distance through farce and irony, an element of lack of control and the irrational seems to be introduced. The opening choice for Marlow is one of either nightmare or reality, but Marlow, while seeking real things and while standing distant from the nightmare, has become part of it, without knowing or seeming to know it, at least, again, consciously. The identification is being made that will destroy detachment and control, which will cause the change in Marlow's relationship to his reader, changing his role as a kind of "moral" guide. Throughout the opening and central stages of the journey, objects float by in the manner of an absurd dream — the gunboat, the wreckage, the detonations, the accountant, the fire, the El Dorado expedition — but Marlow stands to the side and controls through irony and images of low comedy, meanwhile keeping his eyes on his work, on surface reality, and on real things. But while his doing this, in five unclear and dreamlike stages, an identification or kinship which will harm him and destroy him is being created. Thus, one senses that nothing can be done, that, as in the case of all enchantment, this must happen, and that there is something in Marlow which allows this to happen. And if this something in Marlow is in part related to his strong sympathy for and identification with the image of the man alone, Kurtz turning his back on civilization and returning to his station; then a sentimentality coupled with an egoism exists within Marlow who uses an image which suggests a strong level of moral perception and moral choice. Yet there is no clear consciousness of this sentimentality on the part of Marlow. The point is that there is something and that the existence of this something begins to determine what may be Conrad's intention and achievement in his use of an element of comedy in this novel. The threat to control, the roots of all changes — and especially the change in styles with the movement away from low comedy or farce — are apparent from the very beginning.

An identification between Kurtz and Marlow then is established early in the novel. A consideration of every place where Marlow hears about Kurtz or mentions him or reacts to someone else's mentioning him will, I think, show something occurring in Marlow without the conscious control implied by his use of farce and narrative art to view and to present the incidents of his journey. A consideration of the striking image of the enchanted princess in relationship to Marlow's opening image of the silly bird and the serpent will further indicate that this identification — necessary for the "moral shock" he must have — is something which cannot be controlled, something which is part of a dream, the unconscious and not the reality, marked by the task of repairing a wrecked steamer, and, more, by the using of farce and irony. When Marlow describes his nearly fatal illness in terms suggestive of something which belongs in the nightmare world, and in terms suggesting a fall, he possibly gives us something to explain what a choice of nightmares really means, and something to explain or amplify his changes in narrative manner. The diminishing of the use of a comic image on his part is in keeping with his change in general narrative manner, with his description of his illness, with a change in the terms of choice, and an increasing power of the unconscious which undermines what has seemed to be an apparent conscious control. A final scene such as the scene with the Intended, which is a kind of analogue to the whole novel, repeating all its actions and movements, a scene whose confusions are notable, seems another illumination of fall and the fallen state which is Marlow's — for Marlow's responses, in a context of confusions of statements and imagery, of contradictory judgments ,are the responses of a mesmerized dreamer. And an act of control, analogous to a using of irony and farce, the lie, which is imaged as the act of Marlow's pulling himself together, is undermined and destroyed by a failure of awareness, and becomes at most an illusion. Once one perceives the changes and the nature of the changes in Marlow during the journey — which is a movement away from control and conscious ordering — he has then to consider the significance of all conscious control and all protective devices and strategies in the context of a seemingly all powerful unconscious pull, leading to a fall and confusion and "moral shock" which lie at this novel's heart. The questions would be these: Would a comic image, burlesque, or any kind of control, be effective in the type of situation this novel gives us? Might not this control, paradoxically, be dangerous, or misleading because it prevents its user from seeing at once what is really happening to him? (In the parts of *Heart of Darkness* where there is the most control, there is also the least, or the kernel of the least). In other words, as Marlow "sees" what he calls "farce", something happens to him which destroys his ability to "see" this same "farce".

6

But what I primarily wish to suggest here is that there are changes on the level of style in this novel which may indicate changes on the level of being, changes implied by a manner of imaging and the presentation of a final scene — the scene with the Intended — as well as by a manner of creating and establishing kinship, and that what Marlow calls farce is a major factor in our recognition of these changes, as well as in the changes themselves — and that this farce also enables Marlow to do something he cannot do without it, and that, in this last sense, it implies the real mode of salvation, which is not to get involved, which is to keep distance, by not believing or acknowledging that these figures — the pilgrims — are human, by defining them clearly in terms of something, which in this case is disorder and chaos, and by laughing or spitting at them, which is not to take them too seriously. And possibly with all this, there is a change in Marlow's relationship to his auditors and to his readers, a change raising a question about the very use of low comedy, for as he describes scene after scene, and incident after incident, he guides us and defines for us; but as he approaches Kurtz, we begin to look more at him, and he seems to move from without to within. In the same way, the terms of choice change, from a choice between reality and nightmare to a choice between nightmares.

There are now several reasons, it seems to me, why this burlesque, or the "farce" that Marlow makes reference to, has been placed in *Heart of Darkness*. This may be seen in the light of three directions.

(1) This low comedy is made part of a style, and its absence characterizes a change in style, but also, and further, a change in being, which is symbolized in the novel's final episode, in Marlow's sickness, and in a patterning of dark and light images. It also characterizes a change in the relationship between the narrator-artist-arranger and his auditors. It is important in indicating that a change does occur, and, in this sense, exists in relationship to narrative movement, use of imagery in a context of judgment, irony of statement, and what Marlow would call his attention to and upon surface reality, surface truth, and real things.

(2) This low comedy is an act of control, or is part of an act of control. It is a way of preventing involvement, of undercutting significance, or reducing a threat. It and Marlow's farce are reductive and make a judgment in relationship to being reductive, for they negate importance and worth. Also it is part of Marlow's art. It is not only his manner of being "artful" and of protecting himself, but also part of his manner of arranging and ordering his materials. And he does this in relationship to certain controlling images, such as the snake river, the tomb-like city and skeletal white, the dark jungle and the passionate uproar, and the "merry dance of death".

(3) This low comedy is used with a certain type of character, just as it is used by a certain type of narrator-artist-arranger character. It is the defining correlative for the pilgrims in *Heart of Darkness*, or rather for what they represent. And it is the metaphor for their profound disorder. One finds this in the case of villains and fallen men in such works as *Lord Jim*, *Outpost of Progress*, *Victory*. All these characters represent some kind of fall and disorder, and "sordid farce" can become a kind of ritualization of and a giving of form to this disorder. The pilgrims of *Heart of Darkness* seem equated with certain spiritual and moral and psychological conditions, and they are part of the darkness and the evil to be faced. They are unified through their presentation in terms of burlesque; the relationship between all the sin and folly is disorder, and inner chaos. But also the comedy or farce is a reductive process which belittles through dehumanization, and which forces characters into types and rigid gestures, into caricature; and this dehumanizing unifies as well as disorder. Also that much of the comedy is a

comedy of aimlessness and purposelessness and is based upon actions in relationship to consequences is equally significant.[45]

What this all means then, briefly stated, is that the comic image, the
low comedy, of *Heart of Darkness* has an objective and a subjective
use, and that its objective use — to function as a correlative for a
chaotic and dehumanized being — is part of its subjective use, part
of Marlow's attempt to establish a relationship with that which he is
encountering, and part of Marlow's being, his manner of perceiving
and knowing. And this use of a comic image in the context of an
encounter with Kurtz is the source of the realization that what we
really have in this comic image, in this attempt to exercise control
over an experience, is a deception or illusion, of both the possibility
of exercising control and the possibility of moral clarity. Marlow,
faced with a growing self-knowledge and with dangers to himself,
"protects" himself by finding the "right" images for these things
which are dangers to him, and implicit in his idea of using a defense
is the idea of defining what he sees, the idea of the possibility of this
definition. Yet, this faith and trust in a defense is not justified.

---

[45]   This third use needs amplification. There are two literary analogues which
illustrate what is possibly being done in the case of this third use and function
of comedy or burlesque in *Heart of Darkness*. The medieval morality play
with its allegorizations of spiritual and moral states, its vices, had an element
of low comedy or burlesque in its midst. Satan's helpers could often be buffoons. And this buffoonery is kin to a certain kind of evil. Yet there also must
be dangers in bringing together evil and comedy. It can become difficult to
regard the pilgrims or what they represent as real and serious threats, and here
again one seems to return to something that Marlow as character is trying to
do. This threatens to transfer itself to auditor and reader. A second literary
analogue might show that there is and can be a recognition of the importance
of a certain kind of comedy to a certain kind of evil and disorder. In the waste-
lands of *Heart of Darkness*, activity is meaningless and futile — this is proper,
for the disordered person's activity will be meaningless, or rather, part of his
disorder is that he can bring his actions into no kind of relationship to ends and
consequences. The devils of this novel are a bit like those of *Paradise Lost*,
especially in the second book. There they too engage in restless and aimless and
undirected activity, in a landscape of doom, of extremes in climate and topog-
raphy. In *Heart of Darkness*, in a landscape of ravines and hills, of crevices
and rocks, with a fire and the extinguishing of it, with a road and its upkeep,
the shooting at hippo the, the talk of futures and careers, with starched collars,
detonations, and the building of a railroad, there is a similar sense of restless and
useless activity. It is a comedy of reasoning about all things and becoming lost
in wandering mazes.

And it seems to be a type of complacency, for one trusts and rests secure in something when he may not at all be secure. The irony that one uses something to save himself only to fall may be at the heart of Conrad's dark intention, and the novel's theme.

7

The limitations of and irony implicit in the use of a defense or a device of control such as the comic image, which is representative of all the attempts at self maintenance in the novel, and which further represents Marlow's illusions and attempts to maintain "moral" stature, are given an appropriate symbol through an intricate patterning of light and dark imagery. The uses of light and dark throughout the novel might indicate something which will amplify what the establishment of an identification shows, but primarily they are another way of saying what has been said or shown in an examination of the use of "sordid farce" and what it implies. But the movement of light and dark is analogous to the movement from the comic image to daze and all the other movements which are part of this — irony and the illusion of control. In a sense, Conrad has rounded out his novel by tightly integrating imagery and theme. Or rather on the level of the novel's dominant mode of imagery is all that can be found on all other levels. All the explanations are here also.

The recognition is one of complexity. Dowden, for instance, sees the darkness as used on three levels, as the theme of the novel exists on three levels — the darkness surrounding the narrator and his audience, the darkness of the dark continent, and the darkness of Kurtz's degradation, each of these levels being supported by the central image of contrasts in light and darkness. Light, in the figure of the blinding sunlight, is also the perception of the darkness, for darkness is seen in the blinding glare and it is in this blinding sunshine that Marlow first perceives what is to come. The contrast is also used to emphasize the horror of extreme degradation. For another critic — Thrale — the light is also illumination, a kind of grail, Marlow's confrontation with what it is to be human, an illumination which is an effulgence of light. And while Moser sees the unpleasant connotations of whiteness and an association of darkness with truth and vitality, Wilcox goes further and places the whiteness with the white sepulchre and finds sources in *Matthew*.[46]

But there is more to it than this, and the light and dark imagery is to provide an important key to the novel's meaning. Throughout the novel, darkness has been used as a background for the pilgrims, as a background for the journey, as a suggestion of hidden kinship, as the deepest aspect of the human heart and soul, as that which keeps these things hidden, as that which reveals and which is the truth, as a mode of perception, and as that which underlies all light and civilization — the encroaching darkness. The scene with the Intended has illuminated this: the darkness is that which underlies and undermines the whiteness — a whiteness which is both dead and sham, but also purity and unearthliness; the darkness is the quality of Kurtz's "illumination"; the darkness is the identification of the Intended with Kurtz; the darkness is the unknown which is felt in this identification; the darkness is the perception of this unknown and the resultant horror; and the darkness is that which Marlow brings into the parlor with him. Basically, in all this, it may be said to be three things: the truth, or what is learned from the novel's various recognitions and identifications; the perception of this truth; and the mode of the perception of this truth. This darkness is plotted out on the various levels of Kurtz's dark soul, Marlow's, the frame narrator's, and finally the reader's.

Light is used with equal variety and complexity, and perhaps a shade also of ambiguity — something one could also claim for the use of darkness, for that brings forth as well as hides, That which deceives also reveals and that which reveals also deceives; light is both revealer and deceiver. Dowden speaks of the light as the perception of the darkness and sometimes it is so. Even sunlight, however, according to Marlow, can be made to lie. Significant is the scene in Kurtz's cabin — the light in Kurtz's empty cabin. This light illuminates — Kurtz is gone, "moral shock" — and it deceives

---

[46] See Dowden, *Rice Institute Pamphlets*, XLIV, 33-51, and especially 35. See also Thrale, *UTQ*, XXIV, 351, Moser, p. 125, and Wilcox, *PQ*, XXXIX, 1-17.

— Kurtz should be there, "moral shock". This is its irony and ambiguity: the light tells and does not tell.

At the novel's end, as Kurtz approaches death, he tells Marlow that he cannot see, although a candle burns close to his face. For Kurtz, it may be said that the candle or light has no meaning; his darkness is everything and his whole existence, and light could have no value, for his mode of perception is darkness, and darkness is his light. But Marlow needs the light and it is the light which enables him to perceive the darkness. The light is then false here because it is valueless to Kurtz, and true here because it is essential to Marlow. This is analogous to what happens in the empty cabin, where the light is true and where the light is false. The light suggests the security which comes from expectation which is a product of civilization; it presages safety, but one enters and is shocked, and the light illuminates the darkness which is the cause of the shock. A mode of perception carries within itself its own dangers — trust and expectation, and expectation which is parallel to an illusion.

Marlow, then, has light and uses light; Kurtz does not. Marlow is a child of light; this light represents his assurance and his mode of perception. Civilized, he must use civilized modes of perception and express civilized modes of consciousness, implying control, order, and judgment. Kurtz, on the other hand, seems incoherent. This is ironical, I suppose, for Kurtz is carefully presented as a voice. But Kurtz is a child of darkness and he speaks appropriately with what could be called a voice of darkness. He speaks in fragments and disconnected phrases. Because he cannot speak with Kurtz's voice, the voice of darkness, Marlow must speak as best he can in this context, which is to say with the voice of light; but this is inadequate as it had been misleading and deceptive and as it had allowed its user to rely falsely upon it. Basically, there is some kind of limitation contained in a mode of thought and consciousness.

In sum, Marlow encounters the darkness and the heart of darkness. His defenses fail him or fall apart. He is a vastly changed man. He is called upon to see the heart of darkness, but his perception is limited. Yet, this must happen, for he is called upon to perceive the darkness with the eyes and mind of darkness and this he cannot do. Another way of seeing this is to state that Marlow has failed to find the adequate symbol for this darkness, and Kurtz remains, at the most, only half-conceived. Yet, Marlow could do nothing else; his inability to perceive is derived from what may also be called his strength, but which is a flaw in the same sense that his inevitable acceptance of kinship is a flaw. It is something which is just there. Marlow carries with him the truth and a perception — at least partial — of the truth and the experience of these things, but they are not complete, and he is haunted, a victim of the darkness, for while his perception and experience are dark, he could never see in the dark, as he should see in the dark.

Marlow, the child of light, is the civilized European with full consciousness and civilized modes of perception, of control and judgment. His irony, his seeking after incongruities, his detachment and his art — *his use of burlesque and a comic image* — his organizing and arranging — even his "compassion" — are all aspects of this consciousness. He is the best of Europe, while the pilgrims are the worst. As Marlow journies toward the inner station, he journies in the glaring light, and, perceiving darkness and damnation, he condemns them both. Even at the inner station, darkness is perceived and felt in the overhead glare. And some irony is still of use or used, at least. But Marlow suffers a "moral shock". "A light was burning within, but Mr. Kurtz was not there." The context seems apparent — kinship and recognition, but also perception and a mode of perception. For the first time Marlow recognizes, or we recognize and sense, failure and limitation. The light burned but Kurtz was gone. Marlow enters carrying with him the preconceptions of security and the modes of understanding and expectation which are his by European grace, yet, at this moment, the light fails and lies, for Kurtz is not there. Did not something of the same sort happen with burlesque and implications of judgment and control? The shock is one of disappearance and resultant recognition — but the recognition is two-fold, and most important is the recognition of the lie and the failure of the light. Yet, one also must say that the light is true, for it is by the light that Marlow perceives the failure of the light, significant in the disappearance of Kurtz. That what emerges is twofold in this manner is important. A mode of perception — like a defense — has within itself the possibility of failure and fall, when it must encounter the heart of darkness. Likewise, the comic image and the control it implies must be helpless before the increasing impetus of the establishment of a kinship between Marlow and Kurtz, between Marlow and darkness. It appears to be having effect, it appears to be something one can trust; but the last sections of the novel — the sickness of Marlow and the visit to the Intended — show that this is not and probably cannot be the case. And — to return to imagery — throughout, light, again, deceives and reveals — the whiteness of bones and ivory and death reappearing in the image of the dead Fresleven and the spectre Kurtz. But the light is also the sun and the eyes of Marlow. The reader from the very beginning sees an ambiguity here; but the essential analogue does not occur until the scene in Kurtz's cabin, and possibly Marlow realizes this also — thus his "moral shock", or part of it, and his absolute fear.

It is then possible to consider that in *Heart of Darkness* there is not only a journey into self and selfhood, a testing of the individual soul, but also, an inseparable part of this one level of encounter, a second level of encounter, to which the novel's light imagery is a transition, a level of encounter in which a civilization and a cultural tradition are being examined and made to find their darkness. Thus Marlow is not only an individual trying to order the harrowing truths of himself in a certain manner, but also a man using as the basis of this attempt at ordering images and tones which have become part of a sense of scepticism and criticism which are one important strain in European experience. *Heart of Darkness*, in being concerned with Marlow's crisis in his encounter with Kurtz, and Kurtz's crisis in his encounter with the dark forest, is also concerned with the condition of hollowness, with a crisis of Western European civilization. The various characters — Marlow, Kurtz, the pilgrims — define different aspects of the civilization from which they come, different parts in an analysis of civilization, where the darkness is not only some unrestrained savage and primal element in human nature, but also some part of the values and beliefs of a culture which form character and soul. It is to be remembered that in referring to "uncomplicated" savagery, Marlow acknowledges this major distinction between Kurtz and the natives.

The pilgrims are easily dispensed with. They are men for whom civilization means little more than the security of mail and milk deliveries. But Kurtz and Marlow are more problematic. In seeing, for instance what has become of Kurtz in the jungle, one must see what he had been in Europe — a man all Europe contributed to the making of, and a man who is remembered to have been a poet, an artist, a musician, a political orator and force, a humanitarian, a lover, an idealist. In other words, what is the relationship between what Kurtz was and what he has become; in the fact of his being an artist, lover, orator, etc., is there something which explains his being a man that human life is sacrificed to? And in Marlow, with his realism, irony, scepticism, humility, sense of limitations, his restraint, what is the relationship between his light and his darkness? How does this light contribute to his darkness, as how does Kurtz's being all that he was in Europe contribute to his excess, and his lack of a sense of his own limitations, including the final limitation of mortality, which becomes the all-pervading element in Marlow's experience?

Implicit in one tradition of Western culture — its art and belief in subjective individuality, its idealism — is the sense of immortality, limitlessness, excessiveness, and destructive egoism. In a creating element, in other words, lies a destroying element — an identification of saint with satan. And to face the darkness, and the heavy fact of Kurtz, the heavy fact of the combination of the unknown self and what had appeared to be ennobling elements in a civilization, there is Marlow's restraint, his light and all that we see of his manner of perceiving and objectifying subjective experience. Yet this light does not save him, and exactly at the moments when we find him most objective, most detached, at the moments when his light seems strongest, the thing which is to identify him with Kurtz, and to establish a fact of kinship, to bring him to "moral shock", is working. And in some strange way, that Marlow can see a hole in the bottom of a pail, that he can keep his distance, works to blind him to what is happening to him. It is in this fall of Marlow that Conrad's subtlety and irony and tragic sense of human duality, of paradoxes, the sense that the virtues of a civilization paradoxically contain the vices of a civilization, and that these things are too much a part of human consciousness to ever be avoided, are revealed.

8

The concern of this chapter has been a question involving a hole in the bottom of a pail. For this exactly was the problem: in a novel somberly presenting some significant exploration of an inner and an outer darkness, in a journey into self, just what is this very hole in the bottom of a pail doing? It is the contention here that it has relation and great importance, that we may see this pail and this hole leading us to a reading of *Heart of Darkness* by various stages. There are a number of things of this nature in this work, and the outer and central stations are significantly defined by this comic image. This comic image has subjective and objective uses. It is the proper symbol for the spiritual being of the pilgrims and for their disorder, and it is part of Marlow's character — his manner of seeing, knowing, understanding, translating and judging experience, keeping distance, and himself from involvement and kinship with the darkness. As part of his character, it is related to its movements, its modes, Marlow's change in style, his fall and entrance into his own disorder and grove of death. In relationship to his character, its absence strongly implies his fall, and its presence implies its failure. For when it is most clearly evident, an unconscious pull of kinship is operating, and it becomes a contributing factor in this pull, and thus a source of blindness and illusion. And as an illusion, it is part of an all-pervading irony that Conrad uses with Marlow; and as an illusion it is something symbolized by Conrad's use of light imagery, and by the important scene in Kurtz's cabin aboard the river steamer. It ultimately becomes a part of a larger theme in this work, the test of a civilization, the crisis of self coupled with the crisis of that civilization, and a pessimism which sees an inescapable two-sidedness in a saving grace which does not save.

III

BURLESQUE, PARODY, AND ANALOGUE IN *LORD JIM*: A READING OF THE NOVEL*

1

The formal mastery of *Lord Jim* is an acknowledged commonplace of criticism, despite certain objections made to the relative inferiority of the novel's second part, for the novel has been found to be almost musical in its development with a "fugue-like quality of certain scenes, a quality conveyed by dissimilar sequences running parallel in time to each other"; and Conrad has used seemingly isolated fragments and portions of sequences throughout the novel, which he develops through repetition, the sequence eventually becoming clearer and clearer. "This type of narration helps simulate the polyphony of several voices counterpointing each other."[1] Because one of Conrad's purposes is to assault his reader so that he might experience some of the emotional chaos of his characters, he proceeds by the indirect methods of the devices of the narrator and multiple commentator, the illustrative episode, and chronological involution.[2] The last has been especially well treated in recent criticism. Zabel, for instance, discusses the forward-moving chronology of the first three chapters in relationship to what follows. Chapter four involves a wrenching of time — for the possibility of Jim's existing in a forward-moving chronology — a chronology of days and expectations — is forever gone.[3] The

---

* This chapter appeared in shorter form in the *Ball State University Forum*, V (1964), 19-27.

[1] Frederick Karl and Marvin Magalaner, *A Reader's Guide to Great Twentieth Century English Novels* (New York, 1959), p. 50.

[2] Moser, p. 38.

[3] In his introduction to his edition of *Lord Jim* (Boston, 1958), p. xxix. See also Tony Tanner, *Conrad: Lord Jim* (Great Neck, N.Y., 1963), pp. 9-12.

novel deepens "into violent collision with public circumstance",[4] and as Jim meets Marlow, he begins his long effort of justification and recovery, presented through a distorted chronology and repetition — that which describes his ordeal, and the movement back and forth from retrospect to anticipation, from will to action, the conscious self and unrealized identity being brought by this retrospect and anticipation into a redeeming existence.[5] In this light the minor characters of this novel present responses and shared recognitions and serve to illuminate and expand Jim's ordeal, and the recurring incident becomes more than just a *leitmotiv*, for each repetition serves to mark an expanding realization, an advancing penetration of the event and all its causes and consequences.[6] The periphery of meaning will become wider and wider, moving from the personal fate of characters to the fate of society — the world — or moral universe the character inhabits.[7]

The novel not only is made up of, then, the tortuous involutions of understanding and perception, but also works through shifting lenses and double exposures of a sort. The leap, which is one of the things that defines Jim's moral being, is figured and prefigured throughout the novel. In his youth, at the training school, Jim stands *aloof* at the foretop, looking down with contempt, and this is a parallel to his standing on the bridge of the *Patna*. This episode also involves a boat being lowered and a desire to leap — "The Captain of the ship laid a restraining hand on that boy, who seemed on the point of leaping over."[8] The leap recurs throughout as a major theme. The Patusan episode is referred to as a jump; Marlow says, "If he had thoroughly understood the conditions, I concluded, he had better jump into the first gharry he could see and drive on the Stein's house for final instructions."[9] Brown, echoing and perverting Jim's case has the same image — "There

---

[4] Zabel in his introduction to his edition of *Lord Jim*, p. xxix.
[5] *Ibid.*, pp. xxxi-xxxiii.
[6] Zabel, *Craft and Character in Modern Fiction* (New York, 1957), p. 219.
[7] Zabel, *op. cit.*, p. 219.
[8] Here an interesting ambiguity is created, for the leap, which is unrestrained and impulsive, is incidentally directed toward a good action — not the case with the *Patna*.
[9] *Lord Jim*, p. 232.

are my men in the same boat — and, by God, I am not the sort to jump out of trouble and leave them in a d — d lurch. "[10] And the engineer during the *Patna* episode gives this a mock perspective, for he too is defined by a leap, "If I thought I was drunk I would jump overboard — do away with myself, b' gosh."[11]

Guerard has written of *Lord Jim's* method: "The reading of this novel is a *combat*: within the reader, between reader and narrator, between reader and that watching and controlling mind ultimately responsible for the distortions." The novel interweaves and juxtaposes, appeals to judgment and sympathy, to criticism, and to compassion. This becomes its major way of provoking in its readers a strong human response and meaningful conflict.[12] Thus the novel formally perfects itself through the devices of time shifts, central incidents, recurring, defining motifs, multiple perspectives, and ironical juxtapositions. The form parallels meaning. When Jim enters into the dream — Patusan — or into romantic illusion, the style and narrative movement become that of romance. When Jim is struggling — and Marlow too — with moral fact, the style is that of combat.

There is comedy in *Lord Jim*. The major comedy centers about the officers of the *Patna* and is a comedy of description, actions, and expression. For instance, the *Patna* is commanded by "a sort of renegade New South Wales German, very anxious to curse publicly his native country, but who, apparently on the strength of Bismark's victorious policy, brutalised all those he was not afraid of, and wore a 'blood-and-iron' air, combined with a purple nose and a red moustache".[13] This captain, in appearance and gesture, cannot be taken too seriously — he is odious and monstrous, he curses and grunts, wears pajamas and scratches, upsets gharries and is "too thick". His fellow officers are as bad — and as funny. The second engineer is a braggadocio; the chief is described thus:

When he moved a skeleton seemed to sway loose in his clothes; his walk was mere wandering, and he was given to wander thus around the engine-

---

[10] *Ibid.*, pp. 382-3.
[11] *Ibid.*, p. 25
[12] Guerard, *Conrad the Novelist*, p. 153, p. 161.
[13] *Lord Jim*, p. 14.

room skylight, smoking, without relish, doctored tobacco in a brass bowl at the end of a cherrywood stem four feet long, with the imbecile gravity of a thinker evolving a system of philosophy from the hazy glimpse of a truth. He was usually anything but free with his private store of liquor; but on that night he had departed from his principles, so that his second, a weak-headed child of Wapping, what with the unexpectedness of the treat and the strength of the stuff, had become very happy, cheeky, and talkative.[14]

The captain responds; "The fury of the New South Wales German was extreme; he puffed like an exhaust-pipe. ... "[15]

There is comedy in the gestures of the second as he presents himself as one of the "fearless fellows", and he serves as a mock perpective for Jim and Marlow, for it is through the comic act of his falling down that we become aware of the *Patna's* accident, and in gesture he mocks Jim's jump and Brierly's suicide, Jim's contemplation of suicide, his aloofness and contempt, in the same way that the chief engineer's delirium tremens mocks Jim's assuredness that the ship went down. There is also comedy in the captain's meditation (he was biting his thumb, etc.), in his speech on his certificate and the roguishness of all Englishmen, and along with the attempts to free the lifeboat, clearly called by Marlow a burlesque scene, there is an extended moment of comedy in Marlow's visit to the chief engineer at the hospital. There are comic backgrounds (the tourists in the hotel, as Jim and Marlow confer) and comic exchanges (as Marlow talks to Chester — he has a comic vision of Jim on Chester's island). And there is also something comic in the captain of the ship that carries Jim to the mouth of the river Patusan with his malapropisms, in the Dutch resident, and in the grotesqueness of the scene of Gentleman Brown's death:

While he was talking to me in that wretched hovel, and, as it were, fighting for every minute of his life, the Siamese woman, with big bare legs and a stupid coarse face, sat in a dark corner chewing betel stolidly. Now and then she would get up for the purpose of shooing a chicken away from the door. The whole hut shook when she walked. An ugly yellow child, naked and pot-bellied like a little heathen god, stood at the

[14] *Ibid.*, p. 24.
[15] *Ibid.*, p. 24

foot of the couch, finger in mouth, lost in a profound and calm contemplation of the dying man.[16]

a travesty and burlesque of a heroic death picture — the dying hero, and his faithful and mourning attendants, and possibly the fates also.

The comedy here is then a comedy of absurdity in a certain context. It relies upon a background and a tradition, and upon more serious parallels and statements so that its important element is often parody. The situation — a death scene — has certain associations; the tradition of the craft of ship's officer has others. Conrad works heavily with incongruity, but essentially *Lord Jim* is filled with mock gestures and poses; their meaning comes from the situation at the novel's center, as well as from certain established traditions. When the second engineer cries bravery and fearlessness, this can also become comic because we consider the man who is speaking. But also we see this in relationship to the desire for fearlessness on the part of Jim of which it is a parody. And there is always Marlow to draw the comic analogy — a sugar hog's head or a purple nose — it does not matter. But, primarily and most importantly, Conradian comedy in *Lord Jim* is a comedy of actions, of knockabout clowns and slapstick.[17]

2

There are several centers in *Lord Jim* which stand in an analogical relationship to each other: the Marlow-Jim interview, which becomes the center of Marlow's temptation and seeking of self knowledge, and around which the first part of the novel is organized; and the *Patna* episode, which is the center of Jim's temptation (paralleling Marlow's) and which, as such, serves as a center within a center. It is the focal point around which all the various points of view in the novel converge, and its significance is stressed by Jim's desire

[16] *Ibid.*, p. 345.
[17] It is interesting to note that one critic, Moser, has properly remarked that Conrad's treatment of his villains is farcical and heavily ironic and that in *Lord Jim*, "Conrad dehumanizes, mechanizes the evil German captain of the *Patna*, with a comic image reminiscent of Swift's *A Tale of a Tub*." (Moser, p. 27.)

to return to the same spot where he had thought the ship went down, once he is in the lifeboat. Throughout the entire novel, it is the *Patna* episode which monopolizes Jim's thoughts; its importance in Jim's general order of things parallels its importance in Marlow's inner world. But as told by Jim, and as later organized and related by Marlow, this scene is pervaded by a tone and a series of incidents which at first seem strangely placed in a novel dealing with the fate of a man — the tone of low comedy, and the incidents of burlesque. In a sense, the whole *Patna* episode can be regarded as one continuous scene of burlesque.

The burlesque comes primarily from physical slapstick (also to be considered as a kind of spiritual slapstick). The attempts of the ludicrous and dehumanized officers of the *Patna* to get their lifeboat of salvation free and to save their precious skins involve four men "tumbling against each other and sweating desperately over the boat business". The scene is one of extended low comedy:

It must have been a pretty sight, the fierce industry of these beggars toiling on a motionless ship that floated quietly in the silence of a world asleep ... grovelling on all-fours; standing up in despair, tugging, pushing, snarling at each other venomously, ready to kill, ready to weep, and only kept from flying at each other's throats by the fear of death that stood silent behind them like an inflexible and cold-eyed taskmaster. Oh, yes! it must have been a pretty sight.[18]

The first engineer frantically runs back and forth yelling to Jim to "come and help", and at one moment he calls Jim a coward, and at the next it seems he would have kissed Jim's hands. The scene "funny enough to make angels weep" continues:

They were still at that bolt. The skipper was ordering "Get under and try to lift", and the others naturally shirked. ... "Why don't you — you the strongest?" whined the little engineer. "Gott-for-dam! I am too thick" spluttered the skipper in despair.[19]

and so on:

The boat was heavy; they pushed at the bow with no breath to spare for an encouraging word: but the turmoil of terror that had scattered their

18   *Lord Jim*, p. 96.
19   *Ibid.*, p. 101.

self-control like chaff before the wind, converted their desperate exertions into a bit of fooling. ... fit for knockabout clowns in a farce. They pushed with their hands, with their heads, they pushed for dear life with all the weight of their bodies, they pushed with all the might of their souls — only no sooner had they succeeded in canting the stem clear of the davit than they would leave off like one man and start a wild scramble into her. As a natural consequence the boat would swing in abruptly, driving them back, helpless and jostling against each other. They would stand non-plussed for a while, exchanging in fierce whispers all the infamous names they could call to mind, and go at it again.[20]

This burlesque is "enough to make you die laughing", and as Jim stands to the side, the sweating and tumbling officers wrestle with the life-boat, falling back before it time and again, swearing at each other, and suddenly making another rush in a bunch. It is fantastic. Four harlequins (remember how the captain is dressed), sweating and misshapen clowns, spluttering and snapping, rush back and forth, in great confusion, fall, stumble, and kick, and then the scene is punctuated with the death of the third engineer, who, clutching the air, sits down dead — a horrible joke, "hatched in hell". The conclusion involves Jim and the officers in the life-boat and a scene of all threats and no blows, a sham also imaged by Marlow in terms of a "burlesque meanness". The officers look like gutter-drunks, act like animals and foul birds, and talk like chums:

and those two yapping before me like a couple of mean mongrels at a tree'd thief. Yap! Yap! "What are you doing here? You're a fine sort! Too much of a bloomin' gentleman to put his hand to it. Come out of your trance, did you? To sneak in? Did you?" Yap! Yap! "You ain't fit to live!" Yap! Yap! Two of them together trying to out-bark each other. The other would bay from the stern through the rain — couldn't see him — couldn't make out — some of his filthy jargon. Yap! Yap! Bow-ow-ow-ow-ow! Yap! Yap![21]

The officers of the *Patna* are characters of burlesque, personages for the purposes of low comedy, and they are drawn in these terms. The captain is described as —

... extravagantly gorgeous too — got up in a soiled sleeping suit, bright green and deep orange vertical stripes, with a pair of ragged straw slip-

[20] *Ibid.*, p. 104.
[21] *Ibid.*, pp. 117-8.

pers on his bare feet and somebody's cast-off pith hat, very dirty and two sizes too small for him, tied up with a manilla rope — yarn on the top of his big head.[22]

He appears as a "clumsy effigy of a man cut out of a block of fat", and he is imaged as "something round and enormous, resembling a sixteen-hundred-weight sugar-hogshead wrapped in striped flannelette".[23] The absurdity of this man aboard a ship and the total incongruity of his person and actions, reenforcing his physical buffoonery, are continually emphasized — he is referred to as the "thing", as a "bullethead", and as an obscene, "odious and fleshly figure". His legs are like a pair of pillars, his thick carcass trembles from head to foot, and Jim's gorge rises at the "mass of panting flesh from which issued gurgling mutters, a cloudy trickle of filthy expressions. ... "[24] He also meditates by thumb-biting, he thinks all Englishmen rogues, and his fury is immense as he emits sulky grunts and lets loose "a torrent of foaming, abusive jargon", similar to a sewer gush.[25]

This physical description heightens the burlesque and is part of it in the scene where the captain enters his gharry to ride off forever.[26] It is appropriate that the last scene of Jim's temptation and fall should be seen through a comic filter, for the first scene was also viewed in this manner — we know that the *Patna* strikes something through the falling down of the second engineer. The Captain waddles up to the waiting vehicle, jerks the door handle violently, and, in the resulting noise and confusion, almost succeeds in completely overturning the entire gharry — pony, driver, and all. He departs as he appears — and the scene is consistent with his total presentation.

The other officers are comedy caricatures. The second engineer is a mock braggart, and there is something highly unreal, exaggerated, and farcial in both his manner of speaking and his manner of boasting. He brags, "I don't know what fear is", and panics im-

---

[22]   *Ibid.*, p. 37.
[23]   *Ibid.*, p. 38.
[24]   *Ibid.*, p. 24.
[25]   *Ibid.*, p. 22.
[26]   *Ibid.*, p. 46.

mediately; he whines, "If I thought I was drunk I would jump over-board — do away with myself, b'gosh", and staggers accordingly.[27] In his meaningless fight with the half-caste clerk, there is more swaggering, recalling persecuted Donkin of *Nigger of the Narcissus* in his screams that, "He wasn't going to be ordered about." Conrad has reserved, however, his most intense and concentrated use of burlesque for the third most important member of the *Patna* quartet, the chief engineer. He is shown in flight from a marching legion of centipedes:

He burst the door open, made one *leap for dear life* [another mock perspective] down the crazy little stairway, landed bodily on Mariani's stomach, picked himself up and bolted like a rabbit into the streets. The police plucked him off a garbage heap [a mock parallel to Jim's landing in the mud?] in the early morning. At first he had a notion they were carrying him off to be hanged and fought for liberty like a hero. ...[28]

Later on in a hospital ward, he is in great terror as he is positive that many pink toads are lying in wait for him under his bed:

"Ssh! What are they doing now down there?" he asked, pointing to the floor with fantastic precuations of voice and gesture. ...[29]

a fantasia which is further amplified by the comedy of the doctor's interest in the unusual hallucinations of toads and centipedes. "Traditionally he ought to see snakes, but he doesn't. Good old tradition's at a discount nowadays. Eh! His — er — visions are batrachian. Ha! Ha!" And again Conrad, we might note, is using a mock perspective to view a serious theme — the theme of tradition.

Thus, the incident which is central to Jim's experience, and also to Marlow's, is figured in terms of knockabout clowns, in terms of comic types and burlesque meanness; and Jim leaps into a boat which becomes a ship of fools, floundering on a leaden sea. Fur-thermore, this burlesque is a perspective for seeing major themes and aspects of the novel. The chief engineer leaps for dear life down a stairway, the second engineer swears to kill himself, to

[27]   *Ibid.*, p. 25.
[28]   *Ibid.*, p. 50.
[29]   *Ibid.*, p. 52.

jump over the rail, and he falls down as the ship comes to its stop, the officers act out salvation and escape in the crudest of terms, the chief engineer saw the ship go down — he is certain of this — and the doctor speaks of tradition in the context of delirium tremens. There is other comedy in *Lord Jim*, but of greater importance is the major concentration of the comic, the burlesque, which is to be found directing this one scene of the sinking of the *Patna*, and the scene of the telling about it, and the scene which is the retelling about it.

3

The *Patna* episode has its key in the Stein section of the novel, which comes as a dividing chapter between the novel's two major parts, which symbolically relates the one part to the other, and which provides a convenient frame for the action of the Patusan section — Stein's butterflies being the end and the beginning of this part. Stein, in answering questions of being, argues that the task of man (and Jim) is to make the sea, the destructive element, the dream, maintain him. The equation seems reasonably clear. A man that is born falls into a dream like a man falling into a sea — dream equals sea. If he tries to climb out (escape the dream), he drowns. The answer is to submit to the destructive element — the equation is extended and becomes destructive element equals sea equals dream. Zabel has presented the major conflict of the novel — non-being against being — as that of a clash between the values of egotism and the values of ethical fact, or between the dream and its demands and the demands of reality.[30] The Patusan section is an attempt on the part of Jim to make the sea keep him afloat, and it fails for reasons implicit in the *Patna* episode. The temptation in the latter comes from the sea, and Jim's fall is equated with a jump into the sea from a ship which has been described as a little world, or a microcosm. Thus, Jim jumps from the world into the dream (I take Stein's metaphors to be valid for the entire novel) — a jump which can illustrate an example of the failure of being, the

[30] Zabel, *Craft and Character in Modern Fiction*, p. 161.

failure to resolve the conflicts of being.[31]   Instead of plunging into the dream, the unconscious, the illusion, the romantic mist; it would be the hero's task to use his hands and feet to keep himself afloat in these things — to find the proper external symbols or codes which will allow him to bring the dream into a proper relationship to the world, to allow the unconscious to be part of the personality without destroying it.   A man is made up of many things — his basic being involves tension and conflict and his failures are failures of adjustment — his unconscious overwhelms, and the hero stands aloof, paralyzed and incapable of any action. The desire is to jump — to let the sea completely engulf oneself — and this is Jim's failure on ontological as well as psychological levels.

But Conrad is hardly satisfied with the suggestion of a single level of temptation and fall, or rather Jim's fall is identified with many things and implies philosophical as well as moral and psychological levels of interpretation.   The low comedy or "burlesque" that Conrad interjects into this scene, and which Marlow chooses to recall and emphasize is made the appropriate symbol for what Jim's actions imply — morally, philosophically, and psychologically.   It is, in brief, a symbol for disorder, a ritualization of and a giving of form to this disorder, for low comedy involves slapstick, violence, noise — in a word, actions suggesting a rebellion against normal order.   The apparent form of low comedy, the rigid and the mechanical which are basic to this comedy, insofar as they imply a dehumanization and a lack of control, also imply on the level of meaning an essential disorder, an essential formlessness.   And the

---

[31]   This is what C. G. Jung in his *Aion* (London, 1959) calls the dissociation of the personality, which is the root of all neuroses, when the conscious goes in one direction and the unconscious in another — if the contents of the unconscious are not represented to the conscious through symbols or ritual or dogma, not known, in other words, by these symbols, neurosis and catastrophe result. When an inner situation is not made conscious, when the individual is not made conscious of his inner contradictions, the world itself must act out the conflicts and be torn into opposite halves — and this is what happens in *Lord Jim*, where Jim's chaos becomes Marlow's chaos which in turn is transferred to the whole novel, which is the world in this case. For the fullest reading of *Lord Jim* in terms of Jung, see Elliot B. Gose, Jr., "Pure Exercise of Imagination: Archetypal Symbolism in *Lord Jim*", *PMLA*, LXXIX (1964), 137-47.

violent alternations of response, the rushing back and forth, the sweating and the cursing, the costume of the captain all imply this disorder. Furthermore, this is amplified by an identification which appears throughout Conrad's major work and especially in *Lord Jim* and in reference to the *Patna* episode. Certain Conradian characters are imaged as animals, and often these characters are those who create an element of low comedy or "absurd farce" in a particular work. Throughout Conrad's major work a constant identification of the burlesqued with the animal can be noted; Conrad uses animal imagery and animal metaphors extensively, but only within a certain context. The cat, ape, spectre trio of *Victory* arrives at Heyst's island with a bit of play and frolicking arising out of Ricardo's beating of Pedro. Mr. Jones disintegrates into a fantasia at the end of that novel, Schomberg leaps madly, Ricardo snaps and hisses, and the trio travels through the islands with a dime-novel trunk filled with weapons of all sorts. In *Outpost of Progress*, the denouement is filled by the chase and hunt of sweating pigs around an absurd house, And Mr. Verloc of *The Secret Agent* is a reflective beast. *Lord Jim*'s animal imagery is identified with Cornelius, with Brown, with Chester and Holy Terror Robinson, and with the officers of the Patna — all characters of Conradian comedy in one sense or another.[32] The second engineer has the "head of an old horse", the captain is like a "trained baby elephant", he snorts "like a frightened bullock", is called a hound, and growls like a wild beast. The officers together in the life-boat grovel on all fours like beasts, bleating, screaming, howling — and they "screeched together", were like a couple of "mean mongrels", like "three dirty owls". The skipper was "as hoarse as a crow". "He glared as if he would have like to claw me to pieces", "greasy beast", "fishy eyes", "drew in like a turtle": these expressions are all part of the greatest concentration of these similes and metaphors, the scene of the *Patna* catastrophe. (The extent of this mode of imaging is so great as to be almost cloyingly over-obvious — Robinson is a "worn out cab-horse" — Blake of Blake and Egstrom screams in

---

[32] The use of animal imagery can also be a means of creating comedy and comic characters. See my essay "Conrad's Menagerie: Animal Imagery and Theme", *Bucknell Review*, XII (1964), 59-71.

the manner of "an outraged cockatoo" — Cornelius creeps like a repulsive beetle, is mute as a fish, vermin-like, a suspicious cat, a worm, a frightened hen — he also snarls. Brown has fierce crow footed eyes; in his fit, he, bowed and hirsute, claws the air and is like some manbeast of folklore.) Animal imagery is appropriate for these characters and helps to explain their part in low comic actions. For slapstick presents disorder, and an extensive animal imagery clarifies and amplifies this disorder. But most important, these characters, defined by their actions and by the way they are imaged, are a comment on Jim's action. They show us what his action really is, but more also, what has really happened to him; and they are part of the symbolism of the impulsive leap into the sea. The actions of these characters are bestial, instinctive, irrational. That they accompany and direct Jim's leap is to say that the savage, the instinctive, and the irrational accompany and direct his fall. Knockabout clowning is the objective representation of the disorder implicit in this animal regression. In failing to order the unconscious, to order the destructive elements which are part of the dream, in failing to establish a relationship between the dream and the objective world, Jim surrenders to disorder, fails to be, becomes less than human, loses essential form, comes close to the irrational and bestial. These connections are apparent during the lifeboat scene when Jim says: "If I had opened my lips just then I would have simply howled like an animal."[33] And in the analogue to his temptation, Marlow's temptation as he hears Jim's story and his vaporings, the light and dark interview in Marlow's hotel room, Marlow says: "I can't say I was frightened; but I certainly kept as still as if there had been something dangerous in the room, that at the first hint of a movement on my part would be *provoked to pounce upon me*."[34] The fall and the fear of the fall is the fear of the animal, the dehumanized, the mechanical, the wild, the disordered, the unconscious — all part of romantic illusions, dreams, symbolized by the all-pervading sea. It is a fall and fear of fall on various levels.

[33]   *Lord Jim*, p. 124.
[34]   *Ibid.*, p. 171. My italics.

4

A further extension of the implication of this episode is achieved by the suggestion of a morality tradition, where the type character of evil became comic and burlesqued. The *Patna* episode presents, as parts of *Heart of Darkness* did, I feel, some evidence for this suggestion: the deck of the ship is the stage of the morality and also the microcosm, or world; hell lies beneath, in an exact and limited relationship to the deck. The noises from the engine room — the violent slams, the harsh scrapes, the short metallic clangs — are symbols of the disorder below which will soon become the disorder above in the attempts to free the life-boat. Above, it is like the "rest of a troubled dream" — Jim stands aloof, watching. The engineer speaks of the engine room as a hell; he rises from this underworld. His comments about "a fine course of training for the place where the bad boys go when they die"[35] are put into juxtaposition with the image of the *Patna* as a crowded planet speeding through dark spaces,[36] thus causing a suggestion of world to carry over into a suggestion of an underworld. The sea is a static sea, flat, a sheet of ice, like lead; the ship is motionless, the temptation and disorder is the only motion, and above stand the guardian angels (invokers of tradition and order — and Marlow speaks of familiar devils and guardian angels), and the equation is furthered. In giving in to the unconscious Jim gives into the animal, the disordered, and to evil, absolute and transcendental, or so it might seem. This suggestion of a morality tradition superimposed upon an intense and symbolic presentation of a disordered personality enables Conrad and Marlow to approach something like a total view of existence — creates the possibility of a suggestive relationship.

No apparent disunity in terms of structure seems to exist between the various levels; burlesque is the primary device linking all of them, and a device and image characterizing disorder, the animal, and Satan's helpers. Furthermore, Conrad has also the problem of Marlow, which is to interpret Jim, and it is through Marlow

[35] *Ibid.*, p. 22.
[36] *Ibid.*, pp. 21-2.

that Jim is shown to us. Burlesque may be necessary here. For it presents a commentary upon Jim and what has happened to him, a commentary which counterbalances and conflicts with Marlow's inability to come to some final decision and with his alternation between the states of cynicism and sympathy. Possibly, burlesque indicates that unconsciously or consciously Marlow has come to a decision or the illusion of judgment as in *Heart of Darkness* — a deception of narrator and of reader. In any case, burlesque is disorder which is disruptive and out of place in any ordered universe. Its use can be considered to create a major irony in the novel, where there is Marlow's statement of the impossibility of judgment checked by a possible judgment, or the illusion of the possibility of judgment.

The *Patna* episode, which is really the threefold center of the novel — it involves analogical relationships: Jim and *Patna*, Marlow and Jim (and *Patna*), and Reader and Marlow (telling about Marlow hearing about Jim and *Patna*) — then posits a series of conflicts and dichotomies in which burlesque is the central and connecting link. The integrated or ordered personality against the disordered and disintegrated personality is the primary unresolved conflict and tension. Its focus is the leap into the destructive element and the failure to stay afloat. It is Jim's failure to find externals, or a symbolism in the social and real world — the world of community — which will explain and interpret his internal world (tradition is presented, but also mocked, by Conrad, by Marlow). He can find no correlative for his dream; Patusan, which is merely another dream or the dream, only complicates matters by attempting to explain one dream by another, for Patusan is appropriately a land of mists, timelessness, the unconscious, dreams, shifts in light, unreal gestures, peace and secular repose. The irony is that the tradition invoked by the helmsman during the moving scene in court is one possible correlative and one external which would allow one to live with the internal, and yet that even is in doubt, for Brierly dies and Marlow remembers the words of the physician at the hospital. In any case, the pull of Jim's dream seems too much, and his only answer is total immersion, the plunge into unconsciousness and into internal chaos. The second conflict or tension is that between the human and the mechanical, between the human and the bestial. Man is poised somewhere between the angelic and the animal, and he has as his great danger (as he strives to be) not only a disordered self, but something more specific, an animal regression. In all cases, this involves a lapse into formlessness, a formlessness represented by the manner in which Conrad applies his animal imagery in this novel, for a single character may be one moment one kind of animal and the very next moment, another kind of animal. In other words, identified with imagery applied to characters acting in a certain way in relationship to the actions of a main character is a manner of using or applying this imagery. Inconstancy of shape relates to impermanence of being. And again low comedy, with its violent incongruities and gestures and repetitions, serves as the objective representation of this formlessness.

But *Lord Jim* is not only a novel about Jim, but a novel about Marlow. And there is conflict in Marlow which serves as an extension of and analogue to the conflicts within Jim's being — a conflict which is part of Marlow's own attempt at self-definition and discovery, and a conflict which concerns two views about Jim and his actions. Marlow as narrator-artist-character sometimes uses irony and parody in relationship to Jim, and sometimes he uses a diction of compassion and serious involvement and identification. This is to say that low comedy as something remembered and emphasized by Marlow — and which explains something about Jim — may be part of his reaction to Jim, which is part of his attempt to see clearly, to see himself. Thus a symbol for the conflicts within Jim implied in his abandonment of the *Patna* serves as an element in Marlow's response to this abandonment and to Jim, and is an aspect of and the key to his own conflicts and possible disorder.

5

It is Marlow who is telling the story of Jim, and yet he is unable to decide whether Jim's line of conduct was the shirking of his ghost or the facing him out. His final words sum up his total inability to see into the cloud which is Jim's being and experience, as well as his own: "Now he is no more, there are days when the reality of his existence comes to me with an immense, with an overwhelming force; and yet upon my honour there are moments, too, when he passes from my eyes like a disembodied spirit astray amongst the passions of the earth, ready to surrender himself faithfully to the claim of his own world of shades."[37] This is in keeping with Marlow's incapacity to see whether Jim's final act is a moral victory, a redemption, or a further romantic vaporing. One never really knows whether the dream has maintained the dreamer or not.

Throughout most of the novel, one witnesses Marlow responding to Jim; *Lord Jim* is essentially the tale of Marlow, who responds to Jim, and it appears as a form "for presenting the process, feeling, and result of man's quest for knowledge", a knowledge that Marlow is seeking;[38] and in seeking the truth of Jim, Marlow is seeking the truth of himself, then and now as he retells the story, and creates its form. Marlow is uncertain, and he despairs of finalities — rather, he exists, inseparable from unanswerable questions, and he himself suffers Jim's difficulty of not being able to make the proper distinctions between fact and imagination and truth and illusion. The blacks and whites which are distinct in the first part of the novel (although they are given a two-sidedness in use) become confused as Marlow responds more and more intensely to Jim. Patusan is a "crepuscular" place, veiled and clouded, grey.[39]

The novel is Marlow's tale of Jim, and of himself as he responds to Jim and seeks self knowledge. It becomes almost impossible to distinguish between his knowledge of Jim and of himself. The centers of Jim's experience and of Marlow's experience have been noted, and it is exactly at these centers — the chapters concerning the two interviews, in the dining room and in the hotel room — that Marlow's conflict is most pronounced. The whole action of the novel concerns a movement between illusion and fact, between romance and a traditional view of responsibility and reality, between the stranger and the community. And in the sections where Marlow listens and reacts, there is an analogous movement,

[37] *Ibid.*, p. 416.
[38] Tindall, "Apology for Marlow", p. 283.
[39] Tindall, *op. cit.*, p. 282.

focused on Marlow's attitude, which is both cynical and sentimental. Sympathy contends with scepticism, and this is articulated when Marlow claims that Jim appeals to all sides at once — light and dark — and this is shown in action when and as Marlow responds with irony, with sympathy, with comedy, with compassion, with his whole being — always a being in conflict. Marlow is the artist who will leave nothing alone. His face is always changing — his inner self is in flux, and this is parallel to his realization that being itself involves a shifting and flux. The conundrum posed him is simple: how to take Jim and this experience. Marlow unfortunately remains in the dark.

Jim has been tempted and has fallen; Marlow is always on the brink of falling. He is reliving his experiences:

... and with the very first word uttered Marlow's body, extended at rest in the seat, would become very still, as though his spirit had winged its way back into the lapse of time and were speaking through his lips from the past.[40]

and his own discovery:

... as though — God help me! — I didn't have enough confidential information about myself to harrow my own soul till the end of my appointed time.[41]

The appearance of Jim is what first engages him in his conflict, for Jim had no business to look so sound — he is clean and promising, yet Marlow angers because of this "as though I had detected him trying to get something out of me by false pretenses".[42] Throughout, whenever he is about to weaken, to suffer too much involvement, an involvement he fights against as he struggles for understanding;[43] he makes ironical qualifying statements, modifying in one sentence what he has said in another. For instance, he can check a judgment of ideas with an adjective "stupid",[44] or qualify a

---

[40] *Lord Jim*, p. 33.
[41] *Ibid.*, p. 34.
[42] *Ibid.*, p. 40.
[43] A conflict which creates an impossibility, for one struggle tends to weaken him for the other.
[44] *Lord Jim*, p. 44.

statement about man's soul with "— or is it only of his liver?"[45] or say of Brierly's death: "Who can tell what flattering view he had induced himself to take of his own suicide?"[46] but, more particularly, he arranges details in his telling which serve as a defense against this frightening involvement, and which create some distance — he juxtaposes, and creates backgrounds, voices, travellers, and falling teaspoons. The absurd as a background will be part of his perspective of irony. And he verbally responds, pitilessly and cruelly (and he becomes numb and he loses all confidence in himself), with questions and ironically placed choric phrases and ironical repetitions of words that Jim himself has used. In chapter ten, he uses "What a persistance of readiness"[47] to his own advantage, but also he feels a kind of respect, for Jim is on his feet half the night, silent, in the night. He will echo "and be saved",[48] and parody Jim's thoughts as he creates characters parodying Jim's actions. But he feels compassion, and in places the burden of the conflict between compassion and irony is concentrated in the shifting utterances and responses of the man becoming numbed and afraid.

Jim's aspect is two-sided for Marlow:

The mist of his feelings shifted between us, as if disturbed by his struggles, and in the rifts of the immaterial veil he would appear to my staring eyes *distinct* of form and pregnant with *vague appeal* like a symbolic figure in a picture.[49] [emphasis supplied]

and Marlow's response is two-sided for Jim, and for us. Marlow, the artist (Tindall has discussed this role), arranges, but for his own sake as well as for ours. Consistent with this is his use of various perspectives — the placing of one perspective in a violent relationship to another. Mock perspectives — and here low comedy is most important — modify serious ones and serious perspectives modify mock ones; values are never certain, and positions are precarious. Jim's words and romantic poses are seen through the words of an alcoholic chief engineer and the fearlessness of his second. His desire for suicide and rest, parallel to Brierly's actual death (the jump which is a moral failure and a leap into the instinctive and the unconscious is also a leap into death — Brierly's leap, the leap threatened by the second engineer all combine to create the association), is mocked by the gestures of the second engineer on the bridge of the *Patna*. The theme of tradition, eloquent in the voice of the native helmsman, is made ridiculous in the voice of the doctor who is extremely interested in the chief engineer's untraditional hallucinations. The French gunboat officer speaks of fear and honor, and at once Marlow remembers the heroism of little Bob Stanton, who had engaged in a wrestling match with a lady's maid, serving to make the preceding statement of values and heroism look somewhat absurd: "It was for all the world, sir, like a naughty youngster fighting with his mother."[50] While the serious is echoed in the comic, Marlow undercuts and destroys, presents and negates. Even the leap can become a leap onto a garbage can, and Marlow stands, moving back and forth, shifting, seeking and drawing away, indecisive in his response.

His reaction to Stein is of the same stuff. Both the French officer and Stein serve as the physicians and priests of the novel, for they speak absolutely and clearly where no one else does. They both have similarities: they make supposedly clarifying statements about Jim and his action, something which Marlow cannot do, because possibly he sees too deeply, or not deeply enough. Yet, as he undercuts the French officer by a seemingly meaningless digression and juxtaposition, Marlow undercuts Stein by a mode of imagery which emphasizes that Stein too dwells in the mists, that he too disappears into the darkness of an inability of understanding:

He lowered the glass lid, the automatic lock clicked sharply, and taking up the case in both hands he bore it religiously away to its place, passing out of the bright circle of the lamp into the ring of fainter light — into shapeless dusk at last. It had an odd effect — as if these few steps had carried him out of this concrete and perplexed world. His tall form, as though robbed of its substance, hovered noiselessly over invisible things with stooping and indefinite movements ....[51]

[50] *Ibid.*, p. 150.
[51] *Ibid.*, p. 213.

and:

The shadow prowling amongst the graves of butterflies laughed boisterously.[52]

and:

The whisper of his conviction seemed to open before me a vast and uncertain expanse, as of a crepuscular horizon on a plain at dawn — or it, perchance, at the coming of the night.[53]

It is not easy to forget Marlow's abhorrence of mists, or his fascination.

The core then of Marlow's experience is in his interview with Jim and his response to this. He alternates between sympathy and cynicism; he uses protective devices ("for it is my belief no man ever understands quite his own artful dodges to escape from the grim shadow of selfknowledge".[54]) of irony, digression, mock perspectives, and comic images. In a word, then, there is a close relationship between Marlow's movement from sympathy to cynicism and his use of parody to undercut and to raise doubts about the validity of certain truths and values which could apply in the case of Jim as well as in his own case. And this parodic impulse, which leads Marlow to see the leap, the desire for repose, Jim's thoughts on suicide, Jim's wishes and evasions and rationalizations, the theme of honor, and the theme of tradition in the light of a presentation of these things in the context of low comedy, is the key to and the result of Marlow's uncertain self — where he is caught, on the level of knowing, as Jim is caught on the level of experiencing and acting, between various possibilities, with little hope of reconciliation. Marlow's desire to emphasize and dwell upon the low-comic parallels Jim's "desire" to approach that which the low comic represents — disorder. One could almost say that since Jim's actions are vital to Marlow's understanding of himself, Marlow approaches the comic as Jim approaches it, and this approach implies something similar in both cases. Both men find perplexity in their evasions, and the comic in this sense represents Marlow's conflict, while it serves as the central symbol for Jim's

---

[52] *Ibid.*, p. 214.
[53] *Ibid.*, p. 215.
[54] *Ibid.*, p. 80.

disorder. Intellectual Marlow and acting Jim are thus linked together.

6

It is, then, Conrad's achievement that he has taken an episode
and invested it with suggestiveness and complexity, an episode
which is doubled by analogues and recurring motifs, and an episode
which strives to present various dichotomies and tensions, not
united in Jim's or Marlow's being. Conrad does this through his
using of burlesque or images of low comedy as a device which
provides him with the adequate symbol for and commentary on
the disorder implicit in any attempt to be. Burlesque illustrates the
disorder which occurs when the unconscious or the illusion overwhelms, but also the animal and the chaotic, and by linking the
Patna experience to a morality tradition, it defines and clarifies and
judges the former, representing for the reader a traditional evil.
And burlesque is that which connects the various levels of Jim's
fall — the psychological, ontological, and moral — for in the dis-
integration of personality, in the relapse into dehumanized and
mechanical savagery, and in the choice of evil and irresponsibility,
there is one thing in common, and this is shown by knockabout
clowns. But burlesque is more than that, and it is something for
Marlow which it may not be for his auditors,[55] for it is the center
of the action of the novel and the inner movement which seems
to define Marlow as artist and sufferer. It is the focal point around
which his shiftings from detachment to involvement rotate, and it
is part of an elaborate defense against an imminent horror of self-
discovery. Perhaps it is his own tendency towards disorder.
Marlow is subtle, more suble than his auditor can realize. "You
are so subtle, Marlow": this is Marlow's key and motto; he arranges with a purpose which is somewhat veiled. He is holding
fast, or so he thinks. He modifies one view with another; he takes

[55] Although this threat seems to me to exist in all levels of temptation, and
telling also, since the device and commentary are Marlow's — these are the
things he perceives in Jim's fall and in his own being. But more, as he perceives
these things, he also defends himself against them by using burlesque, which
is reductive, and in this use of burlesque is something related to and part of
his urge to parody, which is an urge to undercut (or a compulsion).

wisdom, only to say by digression, or by image, that the wisdom is suspect. If he cannot rely on the French officer or on Stein, he certainly cannot rely on himself — and the reader can see him and also see these movements, contortions, and destructions. Burlesque is a theme, a choice, a temptation. One can tell the story of Jim and of oneself and smile in one's ignorance; this is what Marlow must do. A leap is many leaps, a desire to kill oneself is a wild fantasia; Marlow does not have to interject "and be saved", for he has already created his second engineer. It is to be remembered that this is a telling; it is he who moves from time to time, who has the tortured and torturous response to an experience. He does not know the truth of Jim, or suspects his own knowledge, and at the end, Jim's death can be real or shadowy, for it is uncertain whether he has redeemed himself, or plunged into the sea again. Plainly, the last may even be the act of suicide contemplated throughout — for Marlow is death-conscious and he speaks of the East and the dream and the desire for repose, sometimes images of the death wish. The butterfly floats over the corpses and the leap which is a fall is a leap which is a death desire or wish. But Marlow is confused — he knows that judgment is uncertain and life and conduct shadowy — he, however, can only make Jim the center of his conflict and uncertainty. Jim may be tragic, but tragic perspectives are always balanced by comic ones, and even though a matter of life and death is at hand, one has an apparent choice, which is to view a man's fate through various lenses. Marlow is a romantic and mocks his own romanticism, but the acknowledgment of this romanticism on one level (which causes him to mock) prevents full recognition on another (recognition can only come through this romanticism which is mocked). This concerns involvement. The double must be integrated — loved or hated, but integrated. Yet, one pushes him aside, and Marlow chooses one view and then another.

Marlow says in one place:

... for it is my belief no man ever understood quite his own artful dodges to escape from the grim shadow of selfknowledge.[56]

and this seems to apply to him. Marlow is not only the master of ceremonies and ironist par excellence, but also a pessimist. It is this

[56]　*Lord Jim*, p. 80.

pessimism which seems to direct much of his response to a situation. The reader remembers that Jim thinks in terms of destiny and chances missed, for when he speaks of Gentleman Brown and his crew, he speaks not only of evil men, but of evil destiny.[57] This is the dodge which destroys him. Marlow himself recognizes and emphasizes this falseness of view and attitude. But Marlow, in a manner analogous to Jim's, speaks of destinies and fate and the inevitable, and one wonders how much a truth and how much a dodge this is. It certainly obscures Jim's posturings, but seems to lie at the heart of the exhaustion and negative response which are Marlow's. This is closely related to his undercutting of values. It is not tradition or community that is his final word; rather it is himself, speaking in a voice which knows little except imperishable characters and doom.

Marlow speaks:

As if the initial word of each our destiny were not graven in imperishable characters upon the face of a rock[58]

and on death:

the potent word that exorcises from the house of life the haunting shadow of fate[59]

and on loneliness:

It is as if loneliness were a hard and absolute condition of existence; the envelope of flesh and blood on which our eyes are fixed melts before the outstretched hand, and there remains only the capricious, unconsolable, and elusive spirit that no eye can follow, no hand can grasp[60]

and:

No man could breast the colossal and headlong stream that seemed to break and swirl against the dim stillness in which we were precariously sheltered as if on an island[61]

and:

the struggle without hope[62]

[57]   *Ibid.*, p. 392.
[58]   *Ibid.*, p. 186.
[59]   *Ibid.*, p. 176.
[60]   *Ibid.*, p. 180.
[61]   *Ibid.*, p. 181.
[62]   *Ibid.*, p. 96

and:

It was as if the Omnipotence whose mercy they confessed had needed their humble testimony on earth for a while longer, and had looked down to make a sign ...[63]

and with a pessimism, revealed in a mode of description suggesting loneliness and immenseness:

The riding lights of ships winked afar like setting stars, and the hills across the roadstead resembled rounded black masses of arrested thunder clouds.[64]

This is related to his other "dodges" — his digressions, his irony, his arrangement of parts and episodes, and his telling of the narrative of Patusan, this latter serving as a kind of narrative escape, or escape through narrative, for Marlow in the telling of this enters the mode of romance and becomes submerged in the story for story's sake, which also keeps him from any closer illumination (there is much less emphasis in Patusan on Marlow's responses — Marlow becomes more the narrator, and less anything else here).

Marlow's tone and his use of an imagery of fate and destiny are part of his defense, if also a major aspect of his being. Yet, it is this imagery and tone which come into juxtaposition with the moral (so structured) situation of the novel, a moral situation suggested through the presentation of the *Patna* episode and certain other comments and interpretations on the part of Marlow. These two things put together present a suggestion of choice and no choice. This also Marlow is unable to resolve.[65]

[63]   *Ibid.*, p. 97.
[64]   *Ibid.*, pp. 78-9.
[65]   With all the tensions and conflicts and dodges of the novel, there is the hint of a confusion which is also Conrad's as well as Marlow's. It is not always easy to separate Conrad from Marlow, especially in the hearing of the gloomy voice. The narrator of Chapter two describes the pilgrims boarding the *Patna* in the following manner: "They streamed aboard over three gangways, they streamed in urged by faith and the hope of paradise, they streamed in with a continuous tramp and shuffle of bare feet, without a word, a murmur, or a look back; and when clear of confining rails spread on all sides over the deck, flowed forward and aft, overflowed down the yawning hatchways, filled the inner recesses of the ship — like water filling a cistern, like water flowing into crevices and crannies, like water rising silently even with the rim. Eight hundred men and women with faith and hope, with affections and memories, they had

With all the other tensions and oppositions that this novel posits and creates — the tensions and oppositions of disparate views of a man's actions, of human and dehumanized, of animal and angelic, of ordered and disordered being, of good and evil — the most important to emerge is basically that between choice and no choice,

---

collected there, coming from north and south and from the outskirts of the East, after treading the jungle paths, descending the rivers, coasting in praus along the shallows, crossing in small canoes from island to island, passing through suffering, meeting strange sights, beset by strange fears, upheld by one desire. They came from solitary huts in the wilderness, from populous campongs, from villages by the sea. At the call of an idea they had left their forests, their clearings, the protection of their rulers, their prosperity, their poverty, the surroundings of their youth and the graves of their fathers. They came covered with dust, with sweat, with grime, with rags — the strong men at the head of family parties, the lean old men pressing forward without hope of return; young boys with fearless eyes glancing curiously, shy little girls with tumbled long hair; the timid women muffled up and clasping to their breasts, wrapped in loose ends of soiled head-cloths, their sleeping babies, the unconscious pilgrims of an exacting belief." The style here (the verbal and structural repetitions, the metaphors such as water, etc.) suggests Marlow and differs from the more sober and seemingly controlled sentences of the rest of this chapter. Yet, it is not Marlow who is speaking. The repetitions — "streamed", "came", "filled", etc. — belittle and create distance. There is no paradise, and no hope; and Marlow's mode of presentation pervades everywhere.

A major problem is created with Marlow's pessimism — one can perhaps excuse this by saying that what Conrad is showing us about Jim and his fall is not what Marlow is telling us. The use of burlesque again is ambiguous; in one case, it speaks in terms of clear and absolute values, but in the case of Marlow, burlesque is used to show us his own problem and his conflict. Thus we see from two perspectives, and Jim may speak of destiny and Marlow may speak of fate, Jim may dodge and Marlow may not know — but the reader can know, because Stein speaks and the *Patna* episode has a stage, an understage, and comic buffoons. But these elements have a unity which is more apparent than actual. And the pessimism which is Marlow's extends beyond Marlow (is the narrator of the opening pages one of Marlow's auditors or omniscient narrator Conrad?). I have spoken of a complexity of device and purpose. But the structure and symbol of a morality does not firmly mesh with the novel's other parts — conflicts adding up to unreconciled tension, between conscious forces and attitudes, between unconscious and conscious. Even in the specific scene itself, the pull of the dream, the illusion, and the unconscious seem inevitable, having the weight of destiny and fate. The first level of the fall can be considered to present an evil which does not center upon real choice, but rather upon the inevitable. It is like the perceived evil in *Heart of Darkness*. Yet the traditional morality associations and the staging of the *Patna* episode suggest everyman, tempters, and the possibility of choice. One however, does not choose the integrated personality in the sense that he chooses the right action.

essentially a part of the tension between two views of a man's actions and of the human condition. It is interesting again to note, as Tindall has, that the images of light and dark, clearly plotted and separate in the first part of the novel, become merged and confused in haze and mist in the novel's second part.[66] Choice seems impossible — for Jim, for Marlow, for his auditor. And for Conrad. Conrad weighs one against the other (as Marlow's perhaps unconscious desire for judgment can be said to struggle with his conscious desire to avoid it) — dream against action — morality against determinism. Marlow's pessimism seems more than a "dodge"; it is also a basic concept working throughout *Lord Jim*. In *Lord Jim* the pessimism is related to the dream — the dream may stand for romantic illusion, but it represents also the vital and uncontrolled impulses of being, the pull of the ego toward the glorification of itself. The self versus community — the community is the objective, objective action, and a pattern of order, and as the dream pulls one away from the world of community, so then, the pessimism pulls one away from the world of moral statement, the world of community in another sense. The *Patna* is emphasized as the little world — the sea becomes the romantic dream and the illusion. The problem is to stay aboard the *Patna*, but one has to acknowledge life-boats and pits. Stein speaks of having the sea hold one up; yet, Marlow is not sure (is Conrad?), for he undercuts Stein as the romantic, who is forever in the dark, forever chasing butterflies. His final comment after Jim's death is to refer to Stein's butterflies — romantic mists obscuring all else. The suggestion is one of inevitability — Jim has to jump and jump again, has to do what he does — Marlow feels this, accepts it and rejects it. *He mocks Jim's speech on evil destinies, but also he reacts violently to Jim's statements of choice.*

Conrad, then, through a most suggestive device, balances perspectives and visions, morality, will, and desire — and structural contradictions from the viewpoint of thematic contradictions do not appear as real contradictions. At the very center of *Lord Jim*'s structure, created through burlesque and juxtaposition, is a violent tension between the possibilities of clarity and of obscurity. But

[66] Tindall, "Apology for Marlow", p. 282.

the morality stage of the *Patna* is soon folded up and put away, and Patusan is river journey like that of the Congo. Thus the action and motion and illumination of *Lord Jim* negate moral clarity — the clarity is of another sort, seen through the shifting voices of several romantics, ironical and not so ironical. The novel is about conflict and suffering and tortuous comings and returns — it sees Being in the nature of unresolved conflicts, and this it attempts to make clear through a symbol, becoming theme, suggesting always greater unresolved conflicts.

7

The theme of *Lord Jim*, like that of *Heart of Darkness*, is journey and discovery — the action involves conflict, tension, and impasse. All may be illustrated as follows:

Tension between integrated/disintegrated personality human/animal_____ good/evil	ironic__ comic view of situation/ tragic, compassionate view	involvement/__ detachment	choice and free will destiny and no choice

all unified by conflicts in structure, conflicts between perspectives (second engineer, Brierly, Jim, Doctor, helmsman; Chester, Brierly, Marlow, French officer, etc.), conflicts between language and style (statements of compassion, statements of irony and scorn), conflicts between major images (burlesque and morality stage, dream journey and pessimistic vaporings). The parallel is the way the novel expands outward from one incident, the *Patna* incident:

Patna incident	Jim Marlow	*Patna* Patusan	choice no choice	dream morality

and form is shown not to be distinct from theme and action.

The formal perfection of *Lord Jim* is, then, the perfection of a combat. It is an unfolding from and expansion of an incident which is the center of an action, and the focal point for the novel's various searchings for self knowledge and mastery. The novel has an action; this is the movement of the varied responses of the various characters; it is that which the being of the central character is concentrated upon. It is a movement which is felt and perceived below the level of incidents, and is the essence of these incidents. And low comedy, the major focus for the combat at the center of this novel, exists in the context of other elements reinforcing combat, elements to which it is a key, and to which it is also parallel.

The events of the novel are a series of facts arranged in ordered patterns — they proceed according to plan. The novel is the expansion of an incident. One is to move from the *Patna* episode to Marlow's perception and hearing of the episode, to his telling of it and the reader's perception — an objective movement from one time to another, and in each case a widening of the audience and a concomitant universalizing of the experience. But beneath are tensions and inner movements. The novel presents levels of conflict, ambiguity, tension, and contradiction, levels of combat; as the novel (plot) moves from one level of hearing and understanding to the next,[67] the novel (action) also moves from level to level, expanding, broadening, encompassing all, even aesthetic judgment. The story of Jim begins with Jim encountering the fall aboard the *Patna*, and immediately a series of conflicts are suggested: the overwhelming tensions between romantic idealism and ethical fact, dream and community, integrated and disintegrated personality, human and animal, rational and irrational, good and evil. In this one scene is the perception of the entire novel. For this one scene exists only as Jim speaks to Marlow in a hotel dining room, and as Marlow speaks to his fellow sailors later, and to us; the conflicts here and tensions understood and unreconciled are those the entire novel — of Marlow, of narrator, of reader. Yet the levels of conflict are expanded and the conflicts of the *Patna* episode are subsumed under the conflict between two ways of viewing this episode — burlesque and irony, or tragedy and seriousness — and that is subsumed

[67]   One can speak of plot in two senses: the story of Jim; and the story of the perception of Jim's story. The novel is not only about Jim, but also about Marlow hearing about Jim.

under the conflict between the tenets of choice and the tenets of no choice. This is all finally rounded out by some kind of conflict of judgment which is the reader's. The judgments spiral — we must and cannot judge Jim, we must and cannot judge Marlow, we must and cannot judge the artist (the telling of the tale).

Thus the various levels of expansion of action parallel the various levels of expansion of plot. As one perspective is placed upon another, one telling upon another, so one tension becomes another, and so on, and the reader and all judgment are suspended, hovering delicately between a colossal wrath of forces. The novel is a novel of conflict and contradiction, or impossibility of judgment, the attempt and the repression, the failure and the recognition — each conflict is every other conflict, separate, but analogous; in other words tension exists on all planes: in the being of Jim of Marlow, of the auditor and the reader. It is a presentation of unresolved dichotomies on the levels of action, of judgment of action, and of the judgment of the telling of the judgment of action, levels which are moral, psychological, metaphysical, and aesthetic. The action is directed exclusively to perplexity. The characters have reality and being only from this: that they have and are in conflict, that they are caught in a vast web of inner and outer contradictions, and of "artful dodges". This, too, is the reader's problem, and his definer.

Lord Jim is an exploration of self, of values, of knowledge, and of the possibilities of knowing. What is perceived is that all things are two-sided and unclear, and that absolutes — values and images — must become relatives and doubts. A world is in flux and is uncertain; the Conradian self-discoverer and hero is attacked from all sides and is two-faced himself — he lapses into the agony of not-knowing, he plays one value against another because he must, and he ends with no values, but himself, a voice, the past speaking in the present. The form of this novel is also flux — its mark is violent juxtaposition, and yardsticks judged by other yardsticks, becoming no yardsticks. It sees an experience as full and universal (Jim to auditor), but also it sees that in all possible judgments — psychological, moral, aesthetic — lies the greater possibility of no judgment. Conrad doubles and redoubles, and conflict is imposed upon conflict in the manner of an intricate Chinese puzzle; and yet each

doubling is also individual and necessary, not only because it amplifies and keeps before us an action and our vision, but also because
it says more by introducing an additional sphere of knowing and
judging and experiencing, every time it is extended to cover something new. One starts with an everyman who jumps into a dream
because he lacks the objective sense to make integration possible,
one soon realized that knowing, itself, has its perils and complexities, and one ends with a despair over the possibilities of human
action and a spiritual complacency, obscuring and fighting with
the clarity of morality perspectives.

Lord Jim is a novel of analogues. It is through the repetition of
scenes, of images, of responses, of dodges, that one senses and
feels the movement of the work, which is to be perceived in every
character, scene, speech, and image, almost every word. One is
never allowed to forget or pause; he is — so to speak — surrounded
and entrapped, forced to see, and to see again, and again.

The Stein section, which is the middle of the novel as well as
the link between the novel's two major parts, *Patna* and Patusan,
has just recently begun to get the attention it deserves. It is now
seen that there is more here than just the words of Stein diagnosing
the hero's case and giving the prescription for being. Tindall, again,
one of the most perceptive of Conrad's critics, sees Stein's butterfly
as a central symbol of the novel and as a focal symbol for Marlow,
including, as it does, most of the concerns of Jim and of Marlow —
Jim's ideal, Marlow's Jim, reality and dream, beauty and dirt —
and also as a symbol for the role of Marlow as narrator and artist,
arranging matter. In this latter light, the butterfly is described as
a thing of accuracy and harmony representing the balancing of
colossal forces. Marlow is the artist; not only like the hunter of
butterflies, who is the illusionist, he is also like their creator.[68]
Karl and Magalaner reiterate this, and after some modifications
with slightly less clarity. The butterfly is also an important symbol,
but a symbol of the perfection of nature, of beauty and of delicacy,
and this is opposed to the imperfections of man.[69] These critics —

---

[68] Tindall, "Apology for Marlow", pp. 283-4.
[69] Karl and Magalaner, p. 52. See also Tony Tanner, "Butterflies and Beetles
— Conrad's Two Truths", *Chicago Review*, XVI (1963), 123-140.

Karl and Magalaner — accept Stein as the novel's center and as Conrad's spokesman — for his recognition of the necessity of illusions is balanced by controlled illusions — Jim's illusions not being controlled — and Stein's controlled romanticism detracts from Jim's centrality, offering alternatives to Jim's way.[70] But one wonders if he really is Conrad's spokesman, and if this supposed role of spokesman might not clash with his role as symbol, intellectual symbol for Jim and Marlow (he is as much a symbol as his butterfly). The dividing line between controlled and uncontrolled illusions is not so certain, and it might do well to look more closely at the complex movements and actions of Chapter twenty, especially as they will illustrate more fully what can be illustrated by an examination of the uses of the novel's central comic image.

There are several essential aspects of the Stein chapter, which include not only what is said, but how it is received, and a context or background of imagery and decor. All this movement centers around a butterfly — a very rare butterfly — and the particular peculiarities of its discovery and capture (it is this which is recognized by Tindall, Karl, and Magalaner as the important and controlling symbol). The butterfly is to be seen in the context of Stein's dream of hunting butterflies, and it serves as the beginning and the end of this chapter — "He was going back to his butterflies" — and also as the beginning and the ending of the Patusan section, as its frame:

Stein has aged greatly of late. He feels it himself, and says often that he is "preparing to leave all this; preparing to leave ..." while he waves his hand sadly at his butterflies.[71]

the novel's last words. Diagnosing the problem, Stein articulates the dream-reality conflict: one has to make the dream keep him afloat, one has to live in or with the dream. And Jim will do this or attempt to do this — the leap from the *Patna* is a leap into the sea, which is the figure for the dream, and the journey to Patusan is the journey into the dream, or the second leap. It is also described as a jump, and at its heart is Jim's leap from the stockade. It is a land of timelessness, mists and hazes — and of failure and

[70] Karl and Magalaner, p. 53.
[71] *Lord Jim*, p. 417.

no reality. The butterfly is first perceived hovering over the body of the dead native; it is a shadow, or is first perceived as a shadow. It is captured, once seen, sitting on a small heap of dirt. The identification is butterfly, shadow, death, and dirt. The butterfly is Stein's romantic ideal, or figure for his ideal, for there is also his manner of speech and description. It is unobtainable, the dream, and the greatly desired and sought after, and it is perfection and beauty and delicacy — but it hovers over corpses and rests on dirt. The illusion exists side by side with earth and sordidness and their demands, and it is dangerously close — too close — to death and destruction, Stein's life having just been seriously threatened. The butterfly, itself, is, as Tindall notes, a balancing of colossal forces; and it is exactly in the novel, in the being and hearts of all the major actions and the action, in the characters, that forces are not balanced, for the novel is one of great forces at odds, of great tensions, and the many possibilities of chaos. The butterfly, which represents balance, is the symbol for a romanticism which demands balance — the ideal is integration, to make the dream maintain oneself — yet it is this failure and the split between dream and reality which is the novel's agony, The butterfly is necessity, but irony also. A fragile thing maintains in its being what the souls of men must lack, but also it is the artist or at least the symbol for the novel, for the balancing of colossal forces which is this novel. The novel seems to achieve what the characters do not.

The butterfly exists in relationship to dirt and death. There are echoes throughout Patusan and pre-figurings in *Patna*. The butterfly is Stein's dream: "and even what I had once dreamed in my sleep had come into my hand, too!"[72] and the butterfly "finds a little heap of dirt and sits still on it; but man he will never on his heap of mud keep still".[73] Jim's leap — Chapter twenty-five — from the stockade into the heart of Patusan is a leap into the mud:

This is my second *leap*. I had a bit of a run and took *this one flying*, but *fell short*. Thought I would leave my skin there. Lost my shoes *struggling*. And all the time I was thinking to myself how beastly it would be to get a jab with a bally long spear while sticking *in the mud* like this. I

[72] *Ibid.*, p. 211.
[73] *Ibid.*, p. 213.

remember how sick I felt *wriggling in that slime*. I mean really sick - as if I had bitten something *rotten*. [emphasis supplied][74]

and:

That's how it was — and the opportunity ran by his side, leaped over the gap, floundered in the mud ... still veiled.[75]

Gentleman Brown says to Jim in Chapter forty-one:

I've lived — and so did you though you talk as if you were one of those people that *should have wings* so as to go about without touching the *dirty earth*. [emphasis supplied].[76]

The pile of dirt has become the bog of slime, mud, putrefaction and sickening rottenness — the dirty earth, in a word. Jim's leap is a flying leap and a leap into his dream and illusion; he is the butterfly fluttering above the dirt pile — but he plunges in, into the abhorrent slime. Stein says that man will never keep still upon his heap of mud, and he suggests that the heap of mud is the proper condition of man. Marlow remembers this — the proper condition of man can be felt to be in the slime. Yet there is a great conflict, for man or Jim is butterfly as well as rester in the abhorrent bog; he makes a flying leap, and lands in the mud, but does not stay there. The mud is his entrance into romance. But the butterfly rests upon its pile of dirt and is seemingly satisfied. One must live with dirt and the putrefaction and the demands of the earth — the image is one of resting and balance — the butterfly rests, but Jim leaps. Implying the great forces at work and unreconciled, this is also the identification of the dream with the sordid, romanticism and dirt. Jim makes his entrance via a swamp; Stein finds his desire via a pile of mud.

The butterfly then suggests the romantic dream and illusion, but also Jim, and the man who lives in this, and for this illusion. As dream, it is given a second perspective of dirt, and qualified and judged (suggesting what must happen, possibly making the judgment Marlow would really like to make but cannot). The romantic dream brings irresponsibility and self-deception, and it has dirty hands. But as the figure for Jim — his flying leap, his wings — and

[74] *Ibid.*, p. 251.
[75] *Ibid.*, p. 251.
[76] *Ibid.*, p. 383.

for the man who lives in the illusion, it suggests the natural condition of man (the slime — pessimism gone mad) and the necessity of the illusion (the ennobling — the escape from the slime), but it also suggests that man is always clay and must not forget this. Great forces are at work — the demands of the earth and the demands of the sea. The sea cleanses but also destroys. The romantic ideal is good/bad, enobling/deceiving — beauty is dirt, soaring is landing. The symbol becomes complex; its suggestiveness is overwhelming and focused upon the ambiguities and tensions and prevented judgments which are the core of the novel's action. The symbol contains all that the novel contains.

Furthermore, the leap, which is everywhere in the novel (leap from *Patna*, leap from training ship, leap from job to job, leap into Patusan assignment, leap into Patusan, threatened leap of the second engineer. Brierly's leap, Bob Stanton's leap, Gentleman Brown's talk of a leap, Jim's giving a big jump during the interview in Marlow's hotel room) is not only a leap into romance and a leap into the dream or sea, but also a death, and suggestion of self destruction. The problem is to make the sea maintain oneself, but Conrad, by associating the recurring image of the leap with many things (comic, serious, suicide, ignoble acts, dream, etc.), is able to place this major figure of Jim's experience and the conflict in the novel in the midst of the flux and violent shiftings which define the novel's action. Even the leap is unclear. The butterfly is perceived in relationship to death and putrefaction — its shadow is perceived upon the corpse. The dream and romantic illusion are not only close to the pile of dirt and the bog of slime, but also to the dead man and to death. Brierly's leap is a leap into the sea as is Jim's, but it is a suicide; Jim in the lifeboat contemplates self-inflicted death, and the second engineer combines these two ideas in a third — and in a burlesque — when he speaks of his fearlessness and cries that he would leap overboard and do away with himself. What Jim is, or what he is pursuing is presented in terms of death. The comment on the Patusan experience is provided, and the analogue which contains the conflicting feelings and attitudes and suggestions created. Jim leaps into the heart of Patusan — but he lies in the mud — he has wings and soars, flying, etc. — but he is a shadow and is perceived in death and chill — and danger to self. The danger is Marlow's as he perceives Jim — Jim is his romantic ideal or illusion, or that upon which it is focused; Jim is a shadow for Marlow and is seen only in terms of Marlow's pessimism (mud) and the suggestions of corruption and mortality. The romantic dream is butterfly for Jim; Jim is butterfly for Marlow — in both cases the illusions are to be known only in seeming relationship to death and slime. Marlow provides the judgment of the romantic dream (or his anti-romantic self does), but also he provides us with the sole problem of Jim and himself (leap, romanticism, danger, earth, death), and more complexly the movements or conflicts within himself and possibly Jim's self (sympathy, irony; compassion, cynicism), made clear through the butterfly's position as resting on the dirt and hovering over the corpse, but neither clearly tainted nor clearly untainted. One finds that the flying leap is the exalting of ourselves away from our slime heap, but also the deception of ourselves, for we are basically flesh and dirt, even if we bear wings. The butterfly hovers over and sits upon a pile of dirt; the relationship between the dirt and the butterfly is uncertain. Jim clearly lies in the mud, but also rises above it. This is further suspension of commitment, and only the butterfly itself, balancing forces, leading a section of the novel, defining and not defining all the major characters, remains. It is rare and perfect — the dream, the attained, the magnificant. Unfortunately, Jim is never obtained by Marlow.

Stein seems hardly Conrad's spokesman, and his position, structurally, in the center of the novel, and his role as the one who diagnoses, guarantee nothing. Rather, he is important in relationship to Marlow — the importance of position here is that we get at the novel's middle — and as link between two sections — in a brief space all the major and unresolved conflicts as well as the movement of action of the novel and of the two sections that are linked. One must consider not only what is said here, but how it is received. Marlow is the same man everywhere.

The play of lights and darks and images is the same as that which occurs whenever Marlow must encounter a danger to himself, whenever he sees before him the terror of self-knowledge and self, in a journey up a river, or in a hotel room. He accepts Stein's wisdom, but by his imaging and description, he undermines it, as he undermines all other "absolute" values and remarks. Stein is also a shadow. Stein hears and prescribes, and Marlow describes:

Yet for all that the great plain on which men wander amongst graves and pitfalls remained very desolate under the impalpable poesy of its crepuscular light. ...[77]

and:

We passed through empty dark rooms, escorted by gleams from the lights Stein carried. They glided along the waxed floors, sweeping here and there over the polished surface of the table, leaped upon a fragmentary curve of a piece of furniture, or flashed perpendicularly in and out of distant mirrors, while the forms of the two men and the flicker of the two flames could be seen for a moment stealing silently across the depths of a crystalline void[78]

and:

I saw it vividly [Jim's reality], as though in our progress through the lofty silent rooms amongst fleeting gleams of light and the sudden revelations of human figures stealing with flickering flames within unfathomable and pellucid depths, we had approached nearer to absolute Truth. ...[79]

Emphasized here, in juxtaposition with the direct and clear statements of Stein, are precariousness, quick passage, flames, and shifting forms, formlessness. It is difficult to define with this light.

Chapter twenty moves from dream to reality, from dream to dirt and death, from shadows and evanescent light to clarity, from reaction to reaction, back and forth. It is analogous to the novel's major movements. Superficially, the theme is the conflict between dream and reality; this is the conflict in *Patna* and Patusan; more deeply, it is the conflict between judgment and judgment. In this light, the butterfly stands in a shifting relationship to death and to dirt, for it is good to soar, but one must not forget what it is that one is soaring above. And Marlow fights as romantic and as anti-romantic — he images and stresses to his own purpose, and he reacts to Stein's romanticism by an imagery which suggests a repetition of

[77] *Ibid.*, p. 215.
[78] *Ibid.*, p. 216.
[79] *Ibid.*, p. 216.

his reaction to Jim's. His mode is to state and to counterstate, to hold A up to B and B up to A, to present and to undercut. This mode is operative here; as he had presented the French lieutenant, followed by Bob Stanton; or Jim's words in relationship to the second engineer's or to the chief engineer's; or his own words in relationship to Chester's; he here presents and checks through description and imagery. The spiritual physician is lost in the darkness, and a play of light suggests something which is disembodied and which can never be grasped. As the butterfly is to be seen in some relationship to the corpse and the mud pile, so Stein's words and Stein's being are to be seen in some relationship to shadows and lights, to clouds and vapours. Stein disappears momentarily as Jim had disappeared momentarily in Marlow's hotel room. It is not certain that he could have the controlled romanticism that Karl and Magalaner speak of, for, if he might, then one perceives something that Marlow chooses not to see, or cannot see, because his images suggest little difference between his feeling about Stein and those about Jim, or himself. Marlow is at the center of the novel, and it is he who is important in the Stein section, for he is reacting, arranging, and imaging. It is he who will later stress things which relate to Stein's words on the butterfly — he knows an appropriate and useful symbol when he sees it, and he uses it. Chapter twenty is as much about Marlow as the rest of the novel; the action is that which dictates all being in this novel — conflict and the shifting from perspective to perspective. Caught in a maze created by mist, shadow, flickering light, silence, voices, apparent and false clarity, butterflies and bogs; Marlow tosses from one wall to its opposite. One could say there are many bruises in Chapter twenty.

The levels and movements of this analogue are then the levels and movements of the novel, and they involve conflicts and juxtapositions which we have recognized elsewhere:

(1) romantic dream and illusion-demands of reality (sea-dream/conscious-unconscious)

(2) romantic dream-dirt and death (judgments)

(3) shadows-clear outlines

(4/ Marlow's sympathy-his irony (his romantic and anti-romantic selves — judgments)

Lord Jim is built of analogues and redoublings. It is possible to perceive all its movements and its total action on any one specific level — the centering is always on conflict and missing resolution. The novel is about Jim and about Marlow, and the major movements of Jim's soul and those of Marlow's soul direct and create this book. It is not too far wrong, I should hope, to say that *Lord Jim* is the actions of one man and the mind of another. The inner conflicts and tensions of being and soul, of psyche, have been transferred to the objective world of ordered incidents, which we call plot. *Lord Jim* begins with an incident in Jim's youth that happened aboard his training ship — his contempt, his being on the point of leaping, his failure, his physical station, this in relationship to that of others are prefigurings, (that jump here seems desirable is a further addition to the novel's web of ambiguities and conflicts) of what is to occur later aboard the *Patna*, where he also stands aloof, fails to act, and dreams away. The action between dream and real incident is strong in both cases, but the opening chapter is presented in normal chronology and traditional sequence, for Marlow *is not* involved, and no inner conflicts exists which must direct the arrangement of parts, and there are no moral implications. This first failure is merely an action that does not really go beyond itself, that ends with itself. It is only when Marlow searches, and when actions become involved in greater issues of responsibilities, that chronology is to be destroyed — it is, as Zabel notes, the destruction of an ordered world for Jim, but it is also much more than that.

Most of the *Patna* section of the novel is taken up with the two interviews between Marlow and Jim, where one tells and the other reacts and reveals. The experience for Marlow is a doubling of the experience for Jim. The lighting effects are similar, increasing darkness, the play of dark against the light, and the light against the dark, and the storm. Jim for Marlow is seen as "glimpses through the shifting rents in a thick fog", a mist-man identification which is predominant in Marlow's treating of the romantic dreamer and the illusionist. But more, the conflict of the novel — romantic self against anti-romantic self, or dream against reality — is to be seen not only as the overall movement of the scenes involving

Jim's telling of his story to Marlow, but as the smaller movements which make up this overall movement, the moments of experience comprising the total scene. Marlow's desire to qualify, to repeat and parody Jim's phrases, to punctuate with dashes, and tags, are significant parts of this. Highly concentrated, these conflicts may even reveal their essence in single speeches, as when Marlow speaks of Jim in the life-boat, tiller in hand, and ironically uses "What a persistence of readiness!" (ironical because of what Jim is always saying about being ready) to condemn, only to follow this by a compassionate and milder use of "ready" and a kind of sympathy as he images Jim as a man alone in the night. At the very end of chapter ten,[80] Jim asks Marlow (he is speaking of his con- templation of suicide in the life-boat), "Don't you believe it?" Marlow's answer: "I was moved to make a solemn declaration of my readiness to believe implicitly anything he though fit to tell me", suggests irony, paralysis, seriousness, compassion, terror — in fact, everything. It is a sentence which is the novel's totality.

Jim stands in Marlow's room:

I felt it when he rushed out on the verandah as if to fling himself over [another leap — of course, this has become Marlow's obsession, and part of his irony] — and didn't; I felt it more and more all the time he remained outside, faintly lighted on the background of night, as if standing on the shore of a sombre and hopeless sea.[81]

This is white-suited Jim against the dark, ready to leap, faintly seen, a shadow, by a sea, hopeless and sombre (a sea of lead during the *Patna* episode). Thus, as Jim tells his story, he relives it, and the telling is analogous to the experiencing; and as Marlow hears this, he too experiences, and his experiencing is analogous to Jim's experience, which is analogous to his telling of his experiencing. And when Marlow tells the story of Jim's telling him to his sailor friends and company of auditors, he too relives an important part of his life. Again:

And with the very first word uttered Marlow's body, extended at rest in the seat, would become very still, as though his spirit had winged its way

---

[80]   *Ibid.*, p. 127.
[81]   *Ibid.*, p. 177.

back into the lapse of time and were speaking through his lips from the past.[82]

The point is obvious — Marlow's telling of the story (and the auditor's hearing of it and our reading of it) is analogous to the original incident and its other analogues (analogues of incidents and of relationships). The incidents are doubles and parallels because they contain the same conflicts and directions and movements, each one reflecting the other. Jim seeks himself; Marlow seeks Jim, and himself; Jim has a conflict and tension in being also; Jim does not understand the *Patna*; Marlow does not understand Jim; and so on, and so on.[83]

---

[82] *Ibid.*, p. 33.

[83] The Patusan section of the novel, which ought to contain and double all the conflicts made clear elsewhere, and which ought to become an element, itself, in these conflicts and in the major conflict of the novel if this novel is to be what it seems to be, has been rightly judged inferior. For instance, Karl and Magalaner see it to be so because it (1) lacks a strong central guide, (2) contains unnecessary technical complications, (3) has us see too much of Jim. Moser finds it weak because Marlow or Conrad loses his ironic manner, engages in wooden dialogue, and in the Jim-Jewel chapters, insists upon emotions which he seems unable to dramatize. Guerard finds chapters twenty-two to thirty-five least important, losing depth and appealing to romantic adventure, having nothing to do with the essential Jim, and giving disproportionate attention to the Patusan background, finally emphasizing physical perils at the expense of perils of the soul. In other words, while the Patusan section contains amplifications and analogues (Jim in the mud, etc.) and the whole conflict of dream and responsibility, illusion and reality, judgment and judgment; it lacks the tightness and structural complexity of the novel's first twenty chapters. There is less centering here and a shift in focus, and the one to one relationship of the earlier parts of the novel is weakened and even destroyed. Marlow's symbolic journey is converted into an actual journey up the Patusan — although Marlow's *proper* journey should be in the seeing, and hearing, and the speaking with Jim. Conrad has taken a metaphor and treated it literally.

Furthermore, Conrad or Marlow becomes over-obvious. On occasion, as if to return to the complexity of part one, one finds Marlow recalling light and dark imagery. But this seems superimposed, at times melodramatic, and it merely repeats what has already been made clear.

Nevertheless, Patusan is not all failure, and can be given some artistic justification, for, in one sense, it is the amplification of the problem of the novel and the illustration of Stein's words. Jim is attempting to stay afloat and he enters his dream with a passion. Patusan is a dream world of mist and clouds — people are shapes, appearing and disappearing — the dream is best presented in the manner of a journey, proceeding according to what appears to be more normal chronology. That Patusan is a dream world is

8

Thus everything in *Lord Jim*, a novel which is a complex of analogues, each of which repeats a basic rhythm of tensions and perplexity, reinforces the action of conflict and contradiction; all parts, all characters, all devices and symbols become part of the intricate design of this combat. The low comic image (which one must start

---

suggested not only by its identification with the East, rest, peace, and secular repose, but also by certain other details of importance. It is a place where reality surrenders to shadows, a place of faint hazes, of departures in mists. Marlow's return is described as a return from a dream to reality.

Earlier in the novel, during the *Patna* episode, the East is used as a symbol of irresponsibility, "infinite repose", and "endless dreams". Marlow speaks of Jim's desire of peace (chapter seven) and his yearning for rest, as if Jim wanted to die "in a sort of peaceful trance". This desire for eternal repose is a major temptation and hindrance to action; it hearkens back to Eastern waters with their perfumes, dispensing rest and dreams. Patusan, which is the dream world in its timelessness and shadows, is a land of rest; it is the East and sleep. Jim's dream kingdom and surrogate kingdom (see Zabel) is a kingdom of security, peace, of the peace of the dream. Peace suggests death and stasis, a paralysis; the leap suggests the butterfly, the butterfly the dream, the dream death and decay; the East suggests the dream, and peace which is death. In Patusan, these are all brought together, and the "secular repose" is the corpse, as the land is the dream. And the leap which seems involuntary in the *Patna* episode is desired in Patusan, as the leap of Brierly and the leap of the second engineer are willed, and as they present death (Jim sits in his lifeboat and thinks on death). Death, then, which is implied in the romantic illusion and plunge into the dream, is also a wish and a desire and a dream in itself. Wishing to leap, to immerse himself in his dream, the hero desires (knowingly and unknowingly) repose and annihilation — he sees safety in his greatest peril, which is a denial of being, and the butterfly hovers as a shadow over the corpse and sits upon its pile of dirt; Jim sees neither corpse nor dirt, but Marlow sees and remembers all. Marlow's conflict is that he does see all, and even in Patusan, lacking the tightness and tension of the novel's earlier structure, Marlow can still bring in all the essential movements of the novel — leap, dream, mud, death, desire — to show the contradictions which prevent his judgment. He reacts to Jim's attempt to see things in terms of evil destiny and to Jim's dodges — but he is pessimistic in a way recalling Jim's "evil destiny", and what he views is a journey which is good, is bad, is necessary, is unnecessary. He never knows what Jim's final action is, or whether he faced or shirked. Patusan is the dream, but what shall one say about the dream?

While the one to one relationships of *Patna* are possibly lost in Patusan, Conrad does attempt to imply an analogous relationship between Jim and Marlow of another sort: Jim has plunged into his sea-dream, and Marlow, in telling about this in the manner of a romance, has, in a sense, plunged into his own dream. Both are, remember, romantics; Jim's romanticism is in his ac-

with by asking questions of why — its importance in an organic form), appearing as definer of a scene, as perspective for values, as underminer of values, as anti-romantic check on romantic pretension and as, most important, a perspective amidst many perspectives and a clue to a reading of the novel, is a major element in this combat; and the conflict between attitudes toward Jim, between imagery and statement, as in the Stein chapters, or what is implied in the leap and slime imagery of the Patusan section are evidence of much

---

tions and his journey into Patusan, Marlow's is in his telling about Jim and his journey. He is captured by the telling as Jim is captured by Patusan. Thus, when Jim faces *Patna*, Marlow also faces *Patna* — the world of responsibility and reality and judgment stands against the desire of the illusionist to live the dream; the confusion of Jim is the confusion of Marlow, unconscious and conscious — and when Jim faces Patusan, Marlow also again faces Patusan, only this time the form of this confrontation is a journey rather than a combat and struggle. Furthermore, the telling and the letter emphasizing detail are escapes (as is the illusion); the romantic narration is a further way of preventing judgment and Marlovian responsibility.

Nevertheless, Marlow struggles against the escape and the desire for repose implicit in the romantic manner of narration, for he arranges symbols from the novel's earlier parts and speaks of shadows, darkening night and blood-red skies, of things unclear and unknown. The attempt is to place all of the novel's movements in the final section, but these movements, essential aspects of the combat of the *Patna* section and the Stein section, are somehow lost or not given the prominence which would create the conflict necessary for this section (the conflict between romance and anti-romance on the level of narration). While it might seem proper to have what is happening to Marlow parallel what is happening to Jim, it must also be necessary not to lose Marlow's characteristics as responder and searcher, for that is central to his conflict. In other words, one has to feel and to know that something is happening to Marlow, and that this is important, significant. In this respect, there is too much emphasis on Jim and on Patusan. Marlow is a character who is posed between great forces, unresolved and indecisive, and it is this which defines him. Conrad had to show him plunging into his own romantic dream, but also as a person who has to have some sense of what is happening to him. Jim's blindness in Patusan is made the double of Marlow's blindness in the telling, but Marlow's character involves conscious conflict (at least on several levels), while Jim's involves unconscious conflict. It is exactly this that is lost. The bifurcation which results from having two journeys (actual-symbolic, metaphorical), although made necessary by the demands of the narrator, is unfortunate; and the journey of Marlow up a river to where life stands still and there is no time seems to imply something less than a suggestion of consciousness here. The balance of forces important to the actions and tensions which comprise the action of this novel is missing in Patusan — the elements are there, sometimes successfully, not always so, but not the proper combination of them. Patusan may be analogue, but imperfect analogue.

of the same thing we note in the case of burlesque and parody.

This burlesque is central in the being and consciousness of Marlow. It is often the pivot of shifting responses. The low comedy of the *Patna* episode radiates outward throughout the novel, moving from a specific scene, which it defines, and where it suggests Marlow's judgment of and the possibilities of judgment of Jim's actions and desire for the dream, to the more total experience of Marlow's response to and relationship with Jim. The problem, therefore, concerns a "low comedy" or "farce" or "burlesque" which is emphasized by a narrator-character, Marlow, as he applies it to Jim so that it illustrates something in relationship to both characters, and connects the two as they are connected elsewhere in the novel — the conflict of one amplifying and reinforcing the conflict of the other. A contradiction between the low comic as illustrating something serious about Jim's fall and being part of Marlow's refusal to always see something in this same fall is illusory. The reconciliation is to be found in a metaphor with many possibilities — as related to a recurrent animal imagery, and as related to Marlow's parodic impulse in relationship to the serious themes, actions, desires, and motifs, of Jim's life. And, of course, Marlow's inability to decide about Jim himself is his own particular brand of disorder.

And with all its uses (as defense, as moral definer, as unconscious desire, as view, as source of irony), it becomes an important part of a pattern, part of the defining formal design of this novel — it is no comic relief, no mere section of a morality play, but part of that which in relationship to other things creates and structures the novel. And it is, in this role, not only part of a design and basic form, but also a major aspect of that which engages auditor and reader in this action, in this combat. In any case, there are scenes of low comedy in *Lord Jim*, and the comic becomes something essential in any reading of this novel.

IV

COMEDY IN THE FICTION OF JOSEPH CONRAD:
OTHER WORKS

1. WHEN MARLOW IS NARRATOR

Burlesque, comedy, and farce are the essentials of a two-sidedness, presented and illumined through a pattern of analogues, which unifies *Lord Jim* and, to a certain extent, *Heart of Darkness*. In both cases, the burlesque is something that has objective and subjective uses. The problem of relationship remains, however, a difficult one. The possibilities of moral clarity, often given through burlesque, are scarcely definite in terms of the indecisiveness and incapabilities which plague Marlow as "moral guide". In *Heart of Darkness*, low comedy serves a function similar to that which it serves in *Lord Jim*, for it is a way of imaging certain states of disorder implicit or explicit in certain actions, desires, dreams, choices, states of being, and so on. In part it calls forth a tradition of satanic slapstick. But the general direction of *Heart of Darkness* is towards a snake-like river, and Marlow (the silly bird) moves in a dream, a nightmare, and towards a kinship and a moral shock without awareness and without will. He falls into a kind of hopelessness and apathy; that which appeared as choice at the novel's opening appears as no choice in retrospect. In *Lord Jim*, on the other hand, the inevitability is at times part of Marlow's internal combat and defense, and only partially part of the action, especially if one considers the jump or leap into the dream and unconscious, as well as the voyage to Patusan, the telling of it, and the weight and fascination of Jim's being, as something which can not be prevented. In both novels, images of low comedy are used to suggest possibilities of understanding and clarity (as a metahor for disorder is created) that are lacking in the overall action. At first, burlesque always seems to be more than only Marlow's device and perception. But, as argued earlier, there are, for instance, in *Heart of Darkness* two fairly distinct relationships between Marlow and auditor or reader. He invites us to look at the person he tells us about. It is only later that we begin to look more and more carefully at the teller, and this suggests that the first relationship between Marlow and his auditors is illusory, deceptive, destructive. The implications of the burlesque, low comedy, absurd farce, etc. central to the outer and central stations of *Heart of Darkness* and the scene aboard the *Patna* of *Lord Jim* (or the implications of someone applying a certain kind of imagery, or seeing in a certain way, to the "pilgrims" or to the officers of the *Patna*) must be integrated into the total actions and movements of these novels. This is difficult, since both novels tend towards flux and quickly shifting perspectives, ending with tensions implicit and explicit in the paradoxes which lie at their respective cores.

In both cases, one can argue that seeming contradictions between levels of usage can be resolved through several considerations: in *Heart of Darkness*, the reader moves from a position where there is choice between reality and nightmare to a position where there is only choice between nightmares — in other words, one moves from the possibilities of moral clarity to paralysis. In *Lord Jim*, the possibilities of moral clarity are integrated into the turnings of Marlow's ambiguous confrontation with an ambiguous Jim. They are perhaps suddenly transformed into a part of the tension between will and destiny, judgment and the impossibility of judgment, knowledge and ignorance, sympathy and fear. Even the *Patna* episode itself seems to be several things by virtue of its comic imagery, for the metaphor suggests a two-fold disorder, an evil chosen, and an unconscious plunged into (and this is no matter of choice). Also, the term, or the idea of, *dream* suggests many things.

Both novels have a sense of inevitability in their journeys and confrontations. Even if the opening of *Heart of Darkness* involves a manner of perception involving the possibilities of moral clarity, we are shown Marlow establishing kinship with Kurtz in problem-

atic and mysterious ways. Five steps, Marlow spits, and has an
urgency to reach Kurtz, and an anxiety to see, meet, and talk with
him. This is as if it were being said that this mode of perception,
and what is implicit in the burlesque and low comic image at
first, is part of an illusion and perhaps blameless but destructive
deception, part of the protective devices and complacencies of a
civilization, which are of little value (although they *are* of little
value) as one plunges into a dream. This is part of Conrad's
theme of the best being not good enough, and his theme of the
manysidedness of European light and values. Marlow is attracted to Jim in the same manner; the only difference is that he
struggles.

Marlow is, of course, the user of burlesque and irony, and these
things are basic to his self. Burlesque is a defense and a means of
keeping detachment, and a means of knowing, understanding,
evaluating, and seeing. It is not through his attention to what he
labels "real things" and his work or profession alone that Marlow
"saves" himself, for he can place each phenomenon he sees in a
clear and stable category (or image) through the stressing of the
grossly absurd and farcical elements of the phenomenon. Yet, he
ends confused, even lost. In *Lord Jim*, Marlow is faced with self-
knowledge, knowledge of his own romantic illusions and deceptions,
weaknesses, death desires, indolence, failures, and the potentialities
for more failures. Through a comic image which at first suggested an
assuredness and confidence and, later, an opposing ambiguity and
puzzlement, he attempts to keep a situation of possible horror in
hand (one is certainly aware of another possible way of taking *Lord
Jim*'s scenes of low comedy, and the parodies they lead to — for it
can be argued that something like one's significant actions always
occur in the context of their opposites or in the context of the
absurd, or the problem is to create an image of one's self in ac-
cordance with the absurd — the bad joke — which always sur-
rounds us — but even this is part of an ambiguity related to the
butterfly and dirt, and to the dream and romantic image). Yet
this burlesque and comic image, related to the *Patna* incident, can
proliferate into the various mockeries and parodies of the novel's
central motifs and themes. It is Marlow who stresses the burlesque

elements of the *Patna* episode, of Gentleman Brown's death, of
Chester and Holy Terror Robinson; he feels and sees comic as well
as tragic aspects of a situation. He makes no choice. The comic
then becomes a major factor in this failure or inability to choose,
and ultimately it is a primary source of *Lord Jim's* ambiguities. The
image of Jim's disorder is in some sense the image for the possibilities of Marlow's own disorder.

2. *YOUTH:* THE INNOCENT WORLD

Lacking the multi-sidedness of *Lord Jim* and *Heart of Darkness*,
Youth is still structured by and through analogues and partakes
of the important formal devices of the larger works. In this story,
for instance, there is a combat of a sort also, but one which seems
quickly decided; and there is an irony to be seen when one views
the total work and one to be seen when one starts with the specific
statements of Marlow's telling — in other words, one views from
the outside, from above, and one views from the inside — and the
two movements converge and combine. The center is the conflict
between romance and anti-romance — and a victor is declared,
through context which is directed by anti-romance.

Guerard, contrasting *Lord Jim* to *Youth*, finds some major
difference:

In *Lord Jim*, Marlow is proxy for the intellectual, probing, moralistic
side of a divided self, yet is intimately involved with a side both romantic
and vulnerable. In 'Youth' the division is the ordinary one imposed by
time upon ordinary men; Marlow looks back on the still untested
twenty-year old with some affection and no little irony. But that earlier
self is truly dead. It can be evoked only by the feat of memory, and does
not involve him morally.[1]

but he is wrong in one sense and right in another. Tindall comes
closer to the truth, for he sees three levels in the story rather than
Guerard's two, and the theme of the story is the nature of Marlow,
Marlow who is exposing his own and present sentimentalism as he
exposes youth's sentimentalism: "While old Marlow exposes young

---

[1] Guerard, *Conrad the Novelist*, p. 17.

Marlow to sentimental irony, ironic Conrad, aloof, silent, and
listening among men of affairs, lets innocent old Marlow show old
Marlow up."[2] In *Youth* Conrad and Marlow ironically mock
youthful romanticism and aged sentimentality, which is the successor to that romanticism. But in *Youth*, not as in *Lord Jim*, this
romanticism does not become involved in public act, and no problem of clarity is created, for no moral issues are raised. The theme
of romance opposed to anti-romance is divorced from the spheres
of moral involvement and action, and, in its purity, remains part
of an illustrative journey which eschews the tragic for the comic.
One learns to be cynical and to mock — but this is easily done, for
one's actions and attitudes are merely actions and attitudes: there
is nothing to be betrayed, nothing really to understand. In *Lord
Jim*, Marlow also mocks his romantic self — but this is not complete, for the romantic self is that which brings him nearest to
self-perception (and the comic image which is part of this mocking
of his romantic self is equally as ambiguous) and which leads him
directly to an involvement, from which he cannot see his way
clear to proceed. In other words, the comic image does not exist
in the context of a conflict related to an action of moral significance.
The romanticism which it is opposed to also does not exist in this
context. In the realm of conduct nothing is as certain as in the
realm of comedy (comedy is a part in *Lord Jim*; here it is an all);
the romanticism of *Lord Jim* defines being and leads to consequences not imagined in the briefer story.

   Youth is rich in comedy — it is almost Conrad's most purely
comic work, and certainly it is Marlow's. The comedy is not completely low comedy but a milder kind, that created by improbability,
of juxtaposition, and of expectation. Captain Beard and his wife
flounder in an oarless boat, a saucepan floats by, the captain seeks
his table after the explosion, Marlow is fished out of the hold, the
Judea's crew feast on cheese and ale, the helmsman jumps overboard and swims like a merman, the East speaks in English accents
— and with English curses — the *Celestial* is found looking for
a light, and Abraham goes mad. Even the departure of the rats
from the *Judea*, as detail and as description, is funny:

[2]   Tindall, "Apology for Marlow", p. 278.

Rat after rat appeared on our rail, took a last look over his shoulder, and leaped with a hollow thud into the empty hulk.[3]

It is that last look which does it.

This is the comedy of the improbable. The comic in *Youth* is moreover the defining perspective of the story; it is not one perspective in combat and clash with others, rather it is *the one*, the reality. The romantic ecstasies and rhapsodisings of Marlow as youth are made less than meaningful and a journey which he identifies with one of those voyages "that seem ordered for the illustration of life, that might stand for a symbol of existence",[4] seems really to show nothing and to prove nothing of the kind. The tests and trials and emergencies are too much a part of the general laughter, and Marlow remains the man fished out of the hold with a chain hook tied to a broom handle.

Marlow, mocking his youth and its romantic illusions, arranges and creates juxtapositions. But in his telling, old Marlow shows the romance he mocks (his style showing traits of the romantic and sentimental) and Conrad (or Marlow, Conrad working through Marlow) places the telling in relationship to the comic detail and the sordid anti-romance (actually somewhat good-natured), as Marlow places these latter things in relationship to young Marlow's thoughts and expectations. In other words, young Marlow is placed in a relationship to events and saucepans that parallels the placing of old Marlow's recounting in relationship to the same events and saucepans — the difference, if any, is the following: one involves consciousness and statement, the other, unconsciousness and manner and style of statement. Both however center around a single, clearly defined action and movement — the mocking of the romantic self — and there is no tragedy, no responsibility, no moral involvement — sight is easy, and there is no hedging, no conflict, which is unreconciled, at the deepest recesses of being and a form.

Marlow's style shows the sentimentality and romanticism (and illusion) of a not-too-completely purged old Marlow. He speaks:

---

[3]   *Youth* (Garden City, N.Y., 1927), p. 17. All subsequent references to *Youth* will be to this edition.
[4]   *Youth*, pp. 3-4.

However, they are both dead and Mrs. Beard is dead, and youth, strength, genius, thoughts, achievements, simple hearts — all die. ...[5]

and:

It blew day after day: it blew with spite, without interval, without mercy, without rest.[6]

and:

The old bark lumbered on, heavy with her age and the burden of her cargo, while I lived the life of youth in ignorance and hope. She lumbered on through an interminable procession of days; and the fresh gilding flashed back at the setting sun, seemed to cry out over the darkening sea the words painted on her stern, "*Judea*, London. Do or Die".[7]

and:

The sky was a miracle of purity, a miracle of azure. The sea was polished, was blue, was pellucid, was sparkling like a precious stone, extending on all sides, all round to the horizon — as if the whole terrestrial globe had been one jewel, one colossal sapphire, a single gem fashioned into a planet.[8]

and:

Oh, the fire of it, [youth] more dazzling than the flames of the burning ship, throwing a magic light on the wide earth, leaping audaciously to the sky, presently to be quenched by time more cruel, more pitiless, more bitter than the sea — and like the flames of the burning ship surrounded by an impenetrable night.[9]

and:

He got up painfully, looked at the flames, at the sea sparkling round the ship, and black, black as ink farther away; he looked at the stars shining dim through a thin veil of smoke in a sky black, black as Erebus.[10]

this last followed by Conrad's mocking of this manner of speaking (on another level it mocks young Marlow) through having the captain say, "Youngest first". This is a romantic way of describing; it is young Marlow's manner in old Marlow's telling. The repetitions — "Black, black" — the abundance of appositive constructions, the attempts to give meaning to each scene and detail through

[5]   *Ibid.*, p. 7.
[6]   *Ibid.*, p. 10.
[7]   *Ibid.*, p. 18.
[8]   *Ibid.*, p. 20.
[9]   *Ibid.*, p. 30.
[10]   *Ibid.*, p. 33.

eloquence — the earth and sea as jewel, the ship's motto thrust out as a challenge, the impenetrable night, etc. — the subjective exuberance are part of this romanticism mocked elsewhere by the exaggerations and the positioning of the details of the story. It is as if action purged has become telling unpurged, now in the process of becoming telling purged. The classical allusion, the repeating of "black", "was", "lumbered", the long series, the celestializings belong to the real center of Marlow.

This narration and this manner are put into juxtaposition with comedy, creating a richer comedy, and old Marlow is mocked at the same time that young Marlow is (for they and everything they shall do and say is put against the comic background which then pushed its way into the foreground, becoming the ground reality of this story). This recurs throughout, in reference to young Marlow's hopes and rhapsodies, old Marlow's telling of the story, the details of the story. Marlow tells of his feeling for the ship, his sense of a test, and this is followed by a floating and judging saucepan; Marlow speaks of the jewel-planet and is fished out of the hold, ignominiously. Marlow speaks of a gangway and the merman helmsman:

A portion of several boards holding together had fallen across the rail, and one end protruded overboard, like a gangway leading upon nothing, like a gangway leading over the deep sea, leading to death — as if inviting us to walk the plank at once and be done with our ridiculous troubles. And still the air, the sky — a ghost, something invisible was hailing the ship[11]

but it was only the overboard helmsman:

Someone had the sense to look over, and there was the helmsman, who had impulsively jumped overboard, anxious to come back. He yelled and swam lustily like a merman, keeping up with the ship.[12]

(Notice that the style changes — repeated phrases, series, followed by directness — the two styles parallel the conflict between romance and anti-romance, and since Marlow uses both, either consciously or unconsciously, the conflict and mocking are in him, the old and supposedly more sober Marlow.)

[11] *Ibid.*, p. 26.
[12] *Ibid.*, p. 26.

Youth, like *Heart of Darkness* and *Lord Jim,* develops through and is constructed by analogues and has, as a result, a structural tightness, and a centering of action and a unity, which they also appear to have. The irony of the old Marlow/comic reality situation parallels the irony of the old Marlow seeing the younger Marlow/comic reality situation. Both are analogous — one conflict and irony repeating the other, and both make up one movement — and a clarity is defined by a context which is reality, for the *Judea* is a tub, and there is no getting away from that. Every moment and every movement of youth's illusion and romance and the romantic self is checked by anti-romance and the romantic self is checked by anti-romance and a reality which is the antithesis of romance (made comic to show this clearly — comedy is then one of the poles of the conflict within Marlow between illusion and reality, between romance and anti-romance, but since it is the basic reality, the conflict seems to be resolved in terms of a victory, and comedy's function is to obtain this victory and double purgation).

One expects noble leaps, heroic journeys, a marvelous abandonment of a ship, a heroic arrival in the East; what one gets is fishhooks, cheese and ale, bread and biscuits, and curses — in English — from the bridge of the *Celestial.* The contrasts between Marlow's rhapsodizing and the comic reality, between the *Judea* and the two steamships, between the great chance and the comic ascents, between Byron and the putting out of the fire are all linked in the episode of the arrival of Marlow in the East at the tale's end, where the sea is a dream, where there is a blaze of vivid color, where outlandish craft float by and where three small boats rest with their sleeping men. This episode presents a concluding and powerful contrast and irony which has the East, which is the aspiration of youth, dark as the grave, and the crew sleeping in attitudes of death — so that a place of life is a place of death (the extension of the conflict, its reinforcement).

Only Marlow's final words seem strangely discordant in this action:

... our weary eyes looking still, looking always, looking anxiously for something out of life, that while it is expected is already gone — has passed unseen, in a sigh, in a flash — together with the youth, with the strength, with the romance of illusions.[13]

for they involve a reversal, as if to say that the romance of illusions might be desirable, and as if to suggest that this telling and that journey was the test and the search. But this is the wrong way to view the matter, for one's discoveries are made in the context of Mrs. Beard and saucepans; one is tested without eyebrows before cheese and bottles. Marlow is, however, still the romantic and his final statements are the articulation of something perceived in his style — he has mocked his early romanticism, but has allegiance to it in the form of his older romanticism; and it is Conrad, as Tindall argues, and Marlow (but the unconscious Marlow) who mock both, the final words of Marlow, seemingly discordant in relationship to the action of the work, ultimately standing as ironical and destroying. The comic context is the comment on everything. Avoiding the intricacies of a moral universe, *Youth* harks back to a world without sin. Its form in relationship to what it attempts to do is more perfect; its comedy, less problematic.

Comedy is not only a perspective, but the yardstick of judgment of this short story. Used as the base reality of the world as opposed to the romance of illusions, it is placed into juxtaposition with the words and desires of young Marlow and the narration and romantic narrative manner of old Marlow. No matter what is said, Mrs. Beard and the captain are in their little boat, a saucepan passes by, the rats take one final look and jump (their flight suggesting langour and a kind of comic despair), and the captain and crew feast as the ship goes down. Every posturing and every romantic possibility is immediately checked. Young Marlow seeks all kinds of possibilities for heroic and meaningful experience, but in a world confined by the antithesis of romance and steam, a world where, as Marlow envisages the heroic departure from the sinking ship, Captain Beard and company feast drowsily on cheese and ale. Old Marlow in his recounting, through style, seeks to emphasize the black, black night, and the passing of all things, but he is confined by his own telling, for as he indulges in the excesses of language, he notes that a steamship pulls alongside.

[13]   *Ibid.*, p. 42.

Youth seems almost pure comedy, as pure as it could get in Conrad, a comedy without complications. The story is well integrated, having one focus and a clear unity of ironies. The succession is one of incongruous actions and details — the ship, its name, its cargo, its mishaps, its officers, its Mrs. Beard, its lifeboat without cars, its mad Abraham, its melancholy rats, its explosion, its abandonment. Everything is poised to defeat the purposes of romance — blackened, singed men without eyelashes, the three life-boats with sleeping men in postures of age and death, an Eastern voice crying from the bridge of the *Celestial* for light in English slang, age and death everywhere. The comedy is a device of skepticism, the control upon exuberance, and also the reality,[14] for there is no reality in the story but Marlow, whom we always see and hear, and the reality of the *Judea* and its voyage, the latter the reality of the incongruous, the belittling and the anti-romantic. This episode and this youthful voyage is to reflect (in Marlow's words, *words which he undercuts by his telling*) a great illustration, for there are experiences which will illustrate and explain. One expects this. But the journey suddenly becomes an anti-journey[15] as romance combines with anti-romance (before its defeat on the level of the whole) in the being of Marlow. Marlow or Conrad is making a mockery of the great theme of the significant test, a test which here occurs in a context which must frustrate all tests; and to see this as something illustrative is merely a further delusion of a partially loyal and older mode of romance.

The world is clearly comic (and innocent, for the comic creates the yearning for simplification which steps away from moral responsibility; comedy is an easy, too easy, way to reconcile and resolve the implicit conflicts — in the larger works, *Heart of Darkness* and *Lord Jim*, despite what it implies about this yearning, it is only one element in a multi-element action and form, and it is checked,

---

[14] If the comedy or comic is the reality, does this have meaning in relationship to *Lord Jim*, where one could say that our actions must be performed in the context of the absurd? Does this suggest another meaning or use of the comic image in *Lord Jim*?

[15] The motif of the journey implies certain things, is symbolic, and significant in Western literature and culture; but it is perhaps negated in this story by the telling and its manner (or it is made ambiguous).

accepted, and rejected), and here Marlow dwells upon the incongruities and makes the subtle connections. This is the major element here; this is what is emphasized. And everything said has to be judged in the light of this world, even if the night seems black. Comedy serves a function in the conflict between romance and anti-romance, but unlike in *Lord Jim*, it is also eventually the single judgment, the one and sole perspective by which we view both old and young Marlow and their theme. But, furthermore, comedy is a mocking of the seriousness, pretension, and illusion of seeking great truths in experience, the romance of seeking symbols and exploiting memory. It is difficult to believe that this experience illustrates anything, except its own telling (and it becomes a kind of anti-telling, if that is at all possible).

The comedy of *Youth* is less frenetic, seems more simple, good natured, and is gently absurd. Romance creates few difficulties, so anti-romance and the conflict between the two shall create few problems. This is the comedy of stances exposed. The hero expects and assumes the proper attitude, but the opposite of his expectation occurs (he is never allowed to develop here as he wishes to — his ecstasies, which represent his only letting go, are never dangerous, and held in a tight rein) and the great things one can encounter (storms, fire, sinkings) are perceived through the small (saucepan, fish-hooks, tables). It is sometimes like having a swashbuckling hero enter the stage and swagger — and, pop, his suspenders snap. Even the heroic cliche of rats leaving the sinking ship is reversed — a grand exit of knowledgable rodents. This final gesture — this last look — gives it away. Let us think of Tom Sawyer.

3. *FALK*

Falk, at times, seems to be the other side of *The Shadow Line* and its experience. The stagnant ship, the mad former captain, the sick and strange crew are all aspects of Conradian intitiation and test (the first command theme). But the captain-narrator does not seem essential here (he may be, though, because of the peculiarities of his telling), and this does not appear to be his story — unlike

Heart of Darkness and *Lord Jim*, the emphasis seems placed more upon the man told about (in the sense that the narrator does not consciously feel this is his story in any respect, that he does not point this out to us), and the situation suggested from this.

The theme of *Falk* seems to be that of the primitive passions underlying all codes and all human experience, a theme imaged in a great hunger for food, for woman, for life. The imagery is directed towards the theme. The characters are robed in mythic robes — they are Dianas, and hunters, Centaurs, Olympians, participants in mythic and god-like rapes. Elemental man is attracted to elemental woman in a setting of Cyclopean ruin; pursuit assumes daemonic proportions. And as in *Heart of Darkness* and *Lord Jim*, frame is the foreshadowing and analogue of this, the expansion and extension, for the auditors sit in a setting which suggests primeval man and the eating of flesh.[16]

But, as in *Youth*, the reality, the world, the context of the novel is highly comic and absurd. Exaggeration is important. Conrad wants to bring in respectability, so he brings it in with a vengeance by having the ship *Diana*, not wild but chaste, not the huntress but the hunted, made into a bourgeois German kitchen, garden, and home. The mythic rape of the *Diana* (the wrong *Diana*) is followed

---

[16]   In *Falk*, a work which I think needs far more attention than it has received, Conrad does what he does in *Lord Jim* and *Heart of Darkness* formally. He uses analogues and makes his narrative frame, or situation where a story is told, show the same tensions, movements, and actions of the main story. But in *Falk* — with its three parts or analogues, the sailors dining along the Thames, and thinking of the primitive, Falk's story of the primitive, and Falk and the niece and their actions with suggestions of primitive passion — the formal perfection seems hollow, and the relationship between analogues strange (becoming a source of comedy). That the narrator can image cannibalism and sense the elemental in a fourthrate chop house seems to me comic, especially when one considers that the theme of this tale or novella is undercut throughout by an overwhelming weight of comedy and burlesque. Perhaps there is some mockery of the Conradian narrator's seeking of analogues and significances. There is some further mockery in the variations upon eating and food in this story. For instance, Conrad gives us Schomberg on his table d'hote and also the wretchedness of the food he serves (seen in the context of Schomberg's statements about the food he serves). This suggests the bad food served at the inn in the story's frame. In other words, the eating of human flesh, Falk's story, exists in the context of the bad food served at an inn, the bad food served by Schomberg (and Schomberg talking about his food), and the eating of this food.

by Mrs. Hermann's waving her handkerchief; the narrator goes in
search of Johnson:

It was a very clean native compound: and the big native woman, with
bare brown legs as thick as bedposts, pursuing on all fours a silver dollar
that came rolling out from somewhere, was Mrs. Johnson herself. "Your
man's at home", said the ex-sergeant, and stepped aside in complete and
marked indifference to anything that might follow. Johnson — stood
with his back to a native house built on posts and with its walls made of
mats. In his left hand he held a banana. Out of the right he dealt another
dollar into space. The woman captured this one on the wing, and there
and then plumped down on the ground to look at us with greater com-
fort.[17]

and:

"You've forgotten to apologize", he said at last with extreme precision.
"Not being a gentleman yourself, you don't know apparently when you
intrude upon a gentleman. I am one. I wish you to understand that when I
am in funds I don't work, and now ..."
    I would have pronounced him perfectly sober had he not paused in
great concern to try and brush a hole off the knee of his trousers.
    "I have money — and friends. Every gentleman has. Perhaps you
would like to know my friend? His name is Falk. You could borrow
some money. Try to remember. F-A-L-K-. Falk." Abruptly his tone
changed. "A noble heart", he said muzzily.
    "Has Falk been giving you some money?" I asked, appalled by the
detailed finish of the dark plot.
    "Lent me, my good man, not given me", he corrected, suavely. "Met
me taking the air last evening, and being as usual anxious to oblige —
Hadn't you better go to the devil out of my compound?"
    And upon this, without other warning, he let fly with the banana,
which missed my head and took the constable just under the left eye.
He rushed at the miserable Johnston, [sic] stammering with fury. They
fell,[18]

and witnesses a brawl where the major weapon is a banana; and
the same narrator gets involved in a game of misunderstandings
and confusions, partially manoeuvred by a ridiculous Schomberg,
and framed by the rushing of the hotel crowd to witness the "fight":

But I heard a tumultuous scuffling of boot-soles within. The unspeakable
idiots inside were crowding to the windows, climbing over each other's

---

[17] *Falk*, in the volume *The Nigger of the Narcissus and Typhoon and Other
Stories* (London, 1950), pp. 191-2. All subsequent references to *Falk* will be to
this edition.
[18] *Ibid.*, pp. 192-3.

backs behind the blinds, billiard cues and all. Somebody broke a win-
dowpane, and with the sound of falling glass, so suggestive of riot and
devastation, Schomberg reeled out after us in a state of funk which had
prevented him from parting with his brandy and soda.[19]

Conrad's tale of primitive passions and the elemental man proceeds through the absurd; Diana, who is the niece, is also the ship,
and the ship has curtains. A violent rape is accompanied by flut-
terings of handkerchiefs. The misunderstanding between Falk and
the captain-narrator climaxes in an absurd card game in an absurd
place, surrounded by a comic rushing to see a "fight", following a
journey which ends in a scuffle and the tossing of a banana. Even
the wasteland passed in seeking Johnson is this way — the Australian
beef tin bounding cheerily.[20]

Falk is, then, a tale of primitive passion told on the level of suggested myth, implying the attraction of basic male and female
principles. But in this context, the mythic images are not to be
taken with too much seriousness; the Herculean centaur, a man-
boat (man-beast parody), the moon-like Diana, the rape are all a
bit too much for this setting of Schomberg, Johnson, bananas,
violin-playing captains, knitting mothers, and rag dolls. *Diana*,
too closely identified with the niece-Diana, especially through the
rape, which is a rape of both Dianas, is the epitome of respectability
(the great desire of the mythic Falk)[21] and Diana, the niece-goddess,
just sits there. And the Herculean Falk, man of snow, etc., is shy
and holds back and plays a game of misunderstandings and petty
intrigue. These gods are strangely muted on deck. Only Hermann
occasionally mutters.

This comic context is also to be used in relationship to all suggestions of the narrator's initiation and coming to knowledge. As

[19]   *Ibid.*, pp. 197-8.
[20]   Further comic elements might be such things as Hermann's losing his
slipper (and trying to put it on again) in his rage upon hearing about Falk's
cannibalism, or all of Schomberg's comments and reasons for hating someone,
or the food he serves, his mock philanthropy, and this bad food in relationship
to the other aspects of eating and food in this story, including the tossed banana.
[21]   Much of the comedy of this novella derives from the association of a
"hunger" for respectability with primitive and elementally passionate urges.
The desire for a bourgeois German kitchen is coupled with the antics of a
centaur satisfying his lust — but in a context of a lust for respectability.

in *Youth*, the experience, and the problem, are held up against, are developed against a reality which emphasizes the incongruous, the highly exaggerated, a context which prevents any development. The world goes by with curtains and bananas, absurd characters, and ridiculous words. And whatever is said, whatever is gathered from the experience must be viewed in the light of that world. Falk's story is one of cannibalism; this creates problems not felt in *Youth*, and one again wonders why Conrad has used the backgrounds and contexts he has used. Both in *Youth* and in *Falk* there is a belittling process which prevents us from viewing the experience as the narrator pretends to view it, and which prevents us from taking him too seriously. The great themes of life are not so great — it is folly, Conrad would seem to be saying, to think they are. But in *Youth* it is simply a matter of romantic illusion, detached, isolated from responsibility and action, pure, and by itself. Cannibalism is another matter. The narrator is mocking himself — his tests and crucial experiences contain saucepans and handkerchieves — but in *Falk*, one must take into account that with cannibalism, one is in a suggested world of action and responsibility, and human discovery. Certainly the narrator is discovering the existence of this elemental force underlying everything. No matter though, for the whole theme of cannibalism and the elemental is placed where it is placed — so much so, that Falk's story, once told, does not seem quite so horrible. It is to wonder how seriously we are to take this — this is not to say that Falk is not serious, but that there is a feeling that too much is made of something, that it is not exactly as it might seem. The imagery of gods and goddesses, of creatures of a mythic past frolicking on a deserted Olympian plain cannot be maintained. The *Diana* has too many curtains. The mythic and the elemental are suggested, but it is an absurd elemental, with a man-boat, a ridiculous rape and abduction, an epic battle at cards. Even this will not be maintained:

Her [the niece's] glance was by no means stupid; it beamed out soft and diffuse as the moon beams upon a landscape ... and yet this same glance when turned upon Christian Falk must have been as efficient as the searchlight of a battleship.[22]

---

[22] *Falk*, p. 160.

The goddess is now a battleship.

Even the details of the narrator-captain's own ship seem to be part of this comic reality-context:

I had been appointed ex-officio by the British Consul to take charge of her after a man who had died suddenly, leaving for the guidance of his successor some suspiciously unreceipted bills, a few dry-dock estimates hinting at bribery, and a quantity of vouchers for three years' extravagant expenditure; all these mixed up together in a dusty old violin-case lined with ruby velvet. I found besides a large account-book, which, when opened hopefully, turned out to my infinite consternation to be filled with verses — page after page of rhymed doggerel of a jovial and improper character, written in the neatest minute hand I ever did see.[23]

Totterson wears a mangy fur cap on his head and looks confoundedly stupid, and the old mate snores away at eight, making gross and revolting noises "like a water-logged trombone". But the refuges of the captain-narrator are no better: a domestic ship, which is hardly a ship, more a home, Schomberg's mouth, a miserable table d'hote, and a drunkard beyond a pile of garbage. Conrad, and his narrator, are belittling his theme and his experience; it is being removed from any world of moral responsibility, where it belongs, and from any world of serious involvement. The comic seems an evasion, if not an escape.

The comedy of *Falk*, with its elements of burlesque and even rumor, is a hearkening after an innocence the weight of the story may not bear. It is anti-problem, anti-experience, anti-initiation, the reflection of a strong and frequently unchecked nihilism.[24] In

---

[23] *Ibid.*, p. 153.

[24] Comedy in these works expresses a tendency toward nihilism as well as a yearning for clarity. The nihilism is, of course, implicit in the entire undermining process. That a desire for clarity can be a desire for escape and negation is a further extension of the possibility of ambiguity and two-sidedness in these novels. This implied ambiguity as to the statement of *Falk* is related to an ambiguity at the heart of Conrad's later *The Secret Agent*. This concerns "madness and despair", a phrase which appears to have some great significance because it is often repeated, especially in the last chapter of the novel. *The Secret Agent*, like *Falk*, deals with the elemental, the passions underlying a superficial order and existence, and basically destructive to that order. Stevie — who differs from all the other characters of that novel — is the symbol for this. Winnie discovers or feels this truth, as she abruptly becomes liberated from her prop, from her various deceptions, in order to become a crouching beast, a screaming serpent, the hidden beast revealed. She feels sheer terror and aloneness. This is part of the "impenetrable mystery" that Ossipon is haunted by.

Falk, even with its suggestions of evil, comedy and burlesque are not used with the evil, (except the evil of a failure to understand), but rather purely as defense, with the narrator belittling his experience, and the entire moral issue which could be implied obscured by the clear progression of comic scene and suggestion. If Falk desires respectability, if respectability struggles with the elemental, but they are closely related and tied together, what is one to say about this respectability as it appears in the novel? — A ship with curtains, knitting, children, and hanging clothes? It is shown that the primitive and the elemental which endanger and disorder are not to be feared, are a trifle silly even — but cannibalism is still involved. Even, however, the telling of Falk's story, placed where it is and so told — quickly — is not as terrible or awesome as it might appear under other circumstances. Is Conrad through comedy suggesting a perspective for the momentous moments of our lives where events begin and end with and in themselves, and are totally isolated in themselves, as in *Youth*?

4. THE RETURN, OUTPOST OF PROGRESS, THE SECRET AGENT

The Return, *Outpost of Progress*, and *The Secret Agent* have comic images whose sources differ from those of *Lord Jim*, *Heart of Darkness*, *Youth*, and other Conradian works of conflict and encounter. They all deal with anarchy. *The Return*, which foreshadows *The Secret Agent* in its use of an appearance-reality irony and its almost

---

It is significant that Winnie murders Verloc with the same carving knife Stevie waved about in Chapter three — where, we are told, he would have stuck the German officer like a pig. Verloc, we will recall, is imaged early in the novel as a fat pig. The various discoveries of *The Secret Agent* concern the coming to light of the elemental, which is always there, destroying, corrupting, especially when it is hidden and denied. Possibly it is this force which is the Secret Agent. But this force when brought out into the open, when recognized, remains still destructive. One wonders, when the Professor speaks of "madness and despair" as levers with which to move the world, if Conrad might not be suggesting a possibility of counter-value, of salvation, an opposition to indolence and deadness. But the Professor is an object of Conrad's scorn — having him speak these words must qualify these words. This is so, even if Ossipon remains haunted. Conrad thus makes this suggestion of value and theme ambiguous. Is it a possible solution or value — or another aspect of Conrad's all-pervading irony?

complete dependence upon symbols and development through symbols and central illustrating episodes, is so grim as to be almost a tale of horror, a very dark comedy based upon a multitude of misunderstandings, with implications of grotesquerie and terror, a tale presented through and with a devastating and detached irony which works upon one theme, one idea, creating variation after variation, and climaxing this with an image which contains the whole and which gives it its clearest context. The comedy involves the laughter of surprise as we suddenly perceive that the woman before the mirror is really Satan or death. The comedy is one of misunderstanding, in which one argues from one set of suppositions in such a way as to destroy these suppositions. Passion is applied to non-passion and attack on passion, so that which is opposed to passion becomes passion; and in the frame of a death-corpse city and house, a skull image, reflected in a maze of mirrors, in a house of ill-fame, in a dead city; life and vitality is proven to be death, death appearing as life and vitality. The comedy is one of this transposition. He who is passionate argues against the passion of her who is not, a vast confusion of appearances, the removal of masks. The evil is certainly there — the confusion of life and death to create a living death and a dying life — it is the complex of the misunderstandings and posturings of Hervey and his wife.[25]

Outpost of Progress and *The Secret Agent* present similar visions of total anarchy, where values held dear are meaningless, where relationship is meaningless, where language is meaningless, where all stances, even despair and dying, are meaningless. The tone, pervading here as in *The Return*, is one of ironic hauteur and control,[26] holding the reader at a relatively fixed distance of amused scorn. The particular "chill humor" of *The Secret Agent* is derived from the elevation of passion and suffering to abstraction and from such reduction of the human being to a function or to a formal status (a reductive process which has many other forms and mani-

---

[25] I hesitate to urge the comedy of this novella too much. It is a comedy of a sort, a heavy comedy of false appearances and confusion and misunderstanding. It has many similarities to *The Secret Agent*, especially in its form and its tone — a tone of *hauteur*.

[26] Guerard, *Conrad the Novelist*, p. 226.

festations in Conrad).[27] Conrad is like the narrator of *Falk*, like Marlow at times in *Youth* and *Lord Jim*, but the scorn and mockery are total here. The comedy results when hollow men speak, make love, make revolutions, and die. It is as if Marlow of *Heart of Darkness* has become omniscient author and the "pilgrims" have become major concern.

Outpost of Progress seems a comic *Heart of Darkness* (a parody of its theme as the form of *Falk* seems a parody of its form); it uses the glaring sunshine as a light of illumination and perception, and it speaks of familiar sounds in native voices and the appeal to kinship and complicity. Its subject is a fall into the slavery of slave dealing, a slavery symbolic of the darkness of a metaphysical slavery (in comic and belittling terms) or moral degradation, into scorn, apathy, lust, and lack of control. Carlier even speaks of the necessity of extermination of all "niggers" — when the carcass of the hippo he has shot sinks and floats away.[28] Kayerts and Carlier are completely incompetent and ridiculous. They are imaged as innocent and stupid fools placed in a context and situation which they could never even hope to see. Their voices are meaningless, as they themselves are meaningless. They are children playing games and assuming stances — we are not allowed to forget that these are stances.

Kayerts, having been in the administration of telegraphs, knew how to express himself correctly; the two men, walking arm in arm, think of letting life run easily here.[29] They poke fun at the natives, "Carlier, smoking native tobacco in a short wooden pipe, would swagger up twirling his moustaches and, surveying the warriors with haughty indulgence would say — 'Fine animals.'"[30] They read romantic novels:

Their predecessor had left some torn books. They took up these wrecks of novels, and, as they had never read anything of the kind before, they were surprised and amused. Then during long days there were interminable and silly discussions about plots and personages. In the center of

[27] Guerard, *Od. cit.*, p. 227.
[28] *Outpost of Progress*, in *Almayer's Folly and Tales of Unrest* (London, 1947), p. 108. All subsequent references to this tale will be to this edition.
[29] *Ibid.*, p. 90.
[30] *Ibid.*, p. 93.

Africa they made the acquaintance of Richelieu and of d'Artagnan, of Hawk's Eye and of Father Goriot, and of many other people. All these imaginary personages became subjects for gossip as if they had been living friends. They discounted their virtues, suspected their motives, decried their successes; were scandalized at their duplicity or were doubtful about their courage. The accounts of crimes filled them with indignation, while tender or pathetic passages moved them deeply. ...[31]

and an old paper on "Our colonial Expansion". Carlier and Kayerts read, wondered, and began to think better of themselves and Carlier has a vision of the civilization to come, the civilization he is to bring — quays, warehouses, barracks, *and billiard rooms*.[32]

The fall itself is strongly comic — involving a steady progression as Kayerts and Carlier accept the trade of slaves for ivory, gradually, with rationalizations and weak excuses. The immediate response, a parody of expected reactions, and platitudes, is presented as such with directness:

"We can't touch it, of course", said Kayerts.
   "Of course not", assented Carlier.
   "Slavery is an awful thing", stammered out Kayerts in a nunsteady voice.
   "Frightful — the sufferings", grunted Carlier, with conviction.[33]

Two automatons feel compassion. The abyss and conclusion of the fall is a scene of riot — of burlesque or its suggestion — beginning with an absurd argument and ending with a chase of swollen and porcine figures around a house, where one yells "I'm hit", and the other is dead.[34] The shift is from ironical comments and statements to a single illustrative action — actually the only action of these men — a romp around a house with sweating and groaning.

With Carlier's death and Kayerts' meditation, there is a realization on his part of a new wisdom, but like a comic Adam (or Adam was comic in doing this) he argues about all things, with wrongheaded lucidity.[35] His final action — one of despair — is accompanied by the arrival of the steamboat in a fog, with whistles and bells and puffs of smoke,[36] symbolizing disorder, Kayerts', civili-

[31]   *Ibid.*, p. 94.
[32]   *Ibid.*, p. 95.
[33]   *Ibid.*, p. 105.
[34]   *Ibid.*, p. 113.
[35]   *Ibid.*, p. 115
[36]   *Ibid.*, p. 116.

zation's — it is an action which is mocked, ironical, and yet serious. Kayerts runs to the cross after a non-illumination or anti-illumination, and dies a crucifixion, his tongue out, a purple cheek playfully posed on the shoulder.[37] Kayerts is made a fool even in his despair, and one must consider what and who Kayerts is. The despair and death, following a comic coming-to-truth, ends with a meaningless crucifixion, also mocked in Kayerts' outstretched tongue and his playfully resting cheek. Kayerts' manner of death is a mockery of all he stood for — the story, involving not only the fall of the weak, but also a mockery of the entire process (of the fall), including the death and "redemption" which go with it. The process of finding the truth and of suffering despair is merely a case of loneliness and fear, falsely guised; what Kayerts must undergo is absurd — everything, the trial itself, related to his temptations seems comic. Burlesque enters at the most important moment. Fools can only play at despair. And Conrad has created a mockery not only of the poses of civilization, but of the spiritual poses related to the civilization.

Everything is disordered and chaotic in the story. Civilization comes with whistles and puffs of smoke; it brings brass wires and seeks ivory. Carlier and Kayerts think of a future of billiard rooms and read and cry over romantic literature of passion and escape — they sputter sentiments with strain and mock inarticulateness. They sweat, snap and romp. The shooting of Carlier is a climax of misunderstanding — slapstickish as it appears. And Kayerts is illumined — sees all — like Adam. "He argued with himself about all things under heaven with that kind of wrong-headed lucidity which may be observed in some lunatics. Incidentally, he reflected that the fellow dead there had been a noxious beast anyway. ...."[38] And to the accompaniment of noise he rushes to a cross to be crucified — to die a symbolic death, to be a symbol — to have a "redemption", a redemption for the man (and the age) which cannot be redeemed. Everything is gone — civilization is crude and false; its children are children, in military bearing and sentimental escape; its values are words, repeated mechanically, divorced from

[37] *Ibid.*, p. 117.
[38] *Ibid.*, p. 115.

humanity; its redemptions are the acts of lunatics; and its despairs and its deaths are also poses of despair and death. Kayerts certainly is far from being the crucified man, or any suggestion of any kind of Christ figure. He merely leaps into a final sham and the tale ends in a union of noise, disorder, gesture, and falsity — the steamboat, the fog, the director, the protruding tongue, and the man on the cross.

A macabre comedy which is a "vision of modern life and modern man untouched by grace in any form except that of British legality",[39] *The Secret Agent* is "more nearly a comedy than any other novel of Conrad",[40] and dominant is the element of brutal and sordid farce. *The Secret Agent* is the taking of the "pilgrims" of the officers of the *Patna* and the making of them everything. The world portrayed here is a hellish world, the fire at the central station, expanded and broadened. All is disorder, comedy is appropriate for this, the comedy of quickly perceived incongruities and mocked gestures.[41]

Many of the characters of *The Secret Agent* are absurd and grotesque "as though they expressed in deformity of body a perversity of soul".[42] They are caricatures, like the fat captain in orange striped pajamas, or Holy Terror Robinson in *Lord Jim*. The professor is a good example of this type; he is a man who maintains his superiority by the knowledge that he can blow himself up at any moment he chooses. He has by his extreme extension of ego perfected self-destruction as if he were saying that the ultimate end of self-indulgence and expression was destruction (Conrad is a bit like the professor, but more later), and he is blind

[39]   Guerard, *Conrad the Novelist*, p. 219.
[40]   Hewitt, p. 85.
[41]   Mr. Vladimir, who is mocked, is also the symbol for the mode of mockery, and for the anarchy, the city, and the comedy of the novel. His wit, his corpulence, his connections, his misunderstandings of revolutionaries and their activity make him a symbol containing all the major elements of the novel. As Stevie is the symbol for the form and artistry of the novel, Vladimir is the symbol for its comedy — and as Stevie, by being a half-wit, undercuts the form, so Vladimir, by being what and who he is, undercuts the comedy. Conrad, in other words, allows nothing to remain, even technique and form as a value is destroyed.
[42]   Wiley, p. 107.

irrationality and peevishness asserting their right to define the
moral order, to elevate the instinctual and savage to position of
judge and law-giver. He is absurd because he has elevated a mere
whim and lack of restraint to a heroic stance, because he has pro-
claimed his freedom, his freedom to blow himself up: "But 1 was
thinking of my perfect detonator only."[43]

The Secret Agent is a moral comedy of exposure and reduction.
As in *The Return*, it develops variations upon a theme that non-
anarchy and order are anarchy and that non-loyalty is loyalty; but
in its completeness, going beyond this earlier novel, it creates a
whole world where nothing is as it seems, and where what is, is not.
Everything is its foil, a game of appearances and realities, a death's
head comedy on a greater scale, but again presenting a life which
is death. The novel is built upon and develops through a series of
interwoven themes[44] such as the anarchy inherent in all mankind
and its institutions, a failure to see and a shrinking from explanations, illusion and reality, moral lassitude, themes which are held
together by and perceived through the false relationships, false
understandings, confusions of motives and values which underlie
everything. As in *Outpost of Progress*, there is no redeeming vision
or thought, or suspicion of one, but rather a grouping of postures
and stances, each one mocked and exposed, a mockery which comes
from incongruities and imagery, from juxtapositions which clarify,
from relationships which double and which define in their similarities to other relationships. The comedy proceeds on four levels
simultaneously — the levels of the omniscient narrator's mode of
expression (as in his specific descriptions), of statements made by
characters (Vladimir's discourses), of relationships between characters (Ossipon to Winnie, Heat to Verloc, Michaelis to the Dowager),
and of the entire arrangement of the whole novel, with its contra-
puntal form and its various juxtapositions, where every relationship is held against every other relationship, every scene amplified

---

[43] *The Secret Agent* (Garden City, N.Y., 1953), p. 68. All subsequent refer-
ences to *The Secret Agent* will be to this edition.
[44] See Elliot B. Gose, Jr., "'Cruel Devourer of the World's Light': *The Secret
Agent*", *NCF*, XV (1960), 39-51, D. R. C. Marsh, "Moral Judgments in *The
Secret Agent*", *English Studies in Africa*, III (1960), 57-70, and especially John
H. Hagan, "The Design of Conrad's *The Secret Agent*", *ELH*, XXII (1955), 163.

and defined by its predecessor and its successor (for instance, Winnie-Ossipon in relationship to Winnie-Verloc). The novel uses the set scene, the cinematic close-up and held shot, the still, illustrating, in a kind of *La Ronde* of disorder (character goes to character — Ossipon to the Professor to Heat to Assistant Commissioner to Sir Ethelred, and so forth — A&B to B&C to C&D to D&E, etc.), where form (expressed by circles, recurrences and returnings,[45] where each circle intersects the other — Winnie-Verloc [3 scenes] intersecting Ossipon-Professor [2 scenes] intersecting Heat-Assistant Commissioner [2 scenes] — and where Stevie's circles are the symbol for the form as Stein's butterfly can be said to be a symbol for the form of *Lord Jim*) is, or seems to be, a parody of order, and yet the only order in the novel and its given world.

The Secret Agent is a comedy of false knowledge, of voices in disharmony, of confusion of motives. Everyone misunderstands everyone else — and the novel's last chapter, ending as it does with a refrain of "madness and despair", meaning one thing to Ossipon and another thing to the Professor, is in itself, a statement of gross confusion, where tragedy, guilt, anarchy, real insanity are all brought together as the chorus and the final word. Each circle of relationship based on false knowledge is framed by another circle based on an analogous false knowledge — Ossipon and the Professor serve as the frame for the Winnie-Verloc catastrophe, and it is through their eyes that we perceive it, through their words that we first learn of it (the bomb disaster), and it is through their words later that her suicide (which we learn about during this second Ossipon-Professor interview) becomes as meaningless as everything else. Confusion, illumination, struggle, death — but the world goes on, and Ossipon recalls the newspaper story and walks with guilt, and the Professor calls upon madness and despair to move the world, to prepare for the perfect detonator and the rule of the strong. These things suggest a final incoherence and a rather loud and comic scream.

It is Conradian *hauteur* which leads to the taking of relationships and emotions and the presenting of them in abstract barest form, as valueless and empty. The bedroom scenes between Winnie and

[45]   Hagan, *ELH*, XXII, 148-64, but especially 149-54.

Verloc for instance, are brief and are revealed through a few words in relationship to a few actions and a few sounds — the silence of one of the two, the dark outside, the ticking of the clock, the putting out of the light. But, further, these emotions, and these relationships, are taken and related to seemingly incongruous things, but things which are truly part of them, and which destroy all possibility of belief in them, in this world, at least. Love and passion are mocked through imagery and suggestion relating them to fear, and to madness. There are several love bouts of a sort. Verloc prepares to make love, to coo, on his couch of death, and Winnie creeps nearer in passion, like a beast , in the only passion she is capable of:

"Come here", he said in a peculiar tone, which might have been the tone of brutality, but was intimately known to Mrs. Verloc as the note of wooing. She started forward at once, as if she were still a loyal woman bound to that man by an unbroken contract. Her right hand skimmed slightly the end of the table, and when she had passed on towards the sofa the carving knife had vanished without the slightest sound from the side of the dish. Mr. Verloc heard the creaky plank in the floor, and was content.[46]

After the murder, and in her panic, Winnie encounters Ossipon, and the comedy rises to another crescendo of cross purposes, total misunderstanding combined with extreme passion and feelings, and the two walk arm in arm as any lovers. They engage in two embraces, mock love bouts, with the gestures of one passion and the basis of another. Winnie is even imaged as a serpent, and Ossipon as Eve — a further reversal and confusion of roles (on every level in this novel, roles are confused):

He ceased to struggle; she never let him go. Her hands had locked themselves with an inseparable twist of fingers on his robust back. While the footsteps approached, they breathed quickly, breast to breast, with hard laboured breaths, as if theirs had been the attitude of deadly struggle, while, in fact, it was the attitude of deadly fear.[47]

and:

He rushed forward, groping for her mouth with a silencing hand, and the shriek died out. But in his rush he had knocked her over. He felt her now clinging round his legs, and his terror reached its culminating point, became a sort of intoxication, entertained delusions, acquired the charac-

[46] *The Secret Agent*, p. 215.
[47] *Ibid.*, p. 234.

teristics of delirium tremens. He positively saw snakes now. He saw the woman turned round him like a snake, not to be shaken off. She was not deadly. She was death itself — the companion of life.[48]

In this comedy of cross purposes, of mixed-up emotions and mis-directed passions, of emotions which end in *cul de sacs*; people are not what they seem, and in being so, are, in another sense, what they seem. Worlds get confused, are linked hands around. The images of corpulence and flabbiness rest over everything, defining all roles. Relationships are placed in rigid patterns of recurrence and reversal — Heat meets the Professor in an alley by a symbolic furniture wasteland (confusion and inanimation) and in a few moments positions are reversed; Heat is taken aback, the Professor is taken aback — Winnie talks and Verloc is silent; later Verloc talks and Winnie is silent — and it makes no difference, for from every side and from every angle of vision there is hollowness and chaos. Stevie sets off fireworks and draws circles and circles, the Professor talks about his perfect detonator and madness and despair, so that emotion and value is insane ranting, and formal perfection, the one value left, the wild imaginings of a half-wit. *The Secret Agent* presents *ordered* despair — a very carefully worked out form, giving the appearance of some form and correctness in the form-less void of emotions and relationships in this novel, but the form, its image — a rendering of chaos — comes from the maddened and weakened brain of Stevie — his circles define the novel's form of intersecting and congruent circles, a chaos, becoming a parody of order. In the maze of cross purposes and rigid relationships which have no meaning except its perversion, where every value is reduced through a complex parody (words coming from certain mouths, connections between certain persons), and after the reduction of the possibility of madness and despair, only one value and counter-vision remains, that posited through form — the artist's arranging eye, the reduction of chaos to order, its shaping . But even this last value is undercut, for the form, its image and symbol, come from the incoherent and mad passions of Stevie, and in a specific context, are related to the chaos and absurdities of the revolutionists as they meet at Verloc's. And at the center of the various relation-

[48] *Ibid.*, p. 237.

ships and journeys of this novel is the great personage. The novel
has two poles — the Verlocs and Sir Ethelred, and it moves back
and forth between them. At the end of the movement away from
Verloc and the catastrophe, the movement towards respectable society (the novel moves steadily towards this, then away again, but
the latter movement occurs with a violent wrenching and time shift
— a violent juxtaposition, as if to reinforce, with violence, the links
and relationships which have become horribly clear from the slower
first movement of the novel — from Verloc to Sir Ethelred) is this
"great revolutionary" and his disciple, Toodles:

But, seriously, you can't imagine how irritated he is by the attacks on
his Bill for the nationalization of Fisheries. They call it the beginning
of social revolution. Of course, it is a revolutionary measure. ...[49]

and:

This fight takes it out of him frightfully. The man's getting exhausted. I
feel it by the way he leans on my arm as we walk over. And, I say, is he
safe in the streets? Mullens has been marching his men up here this
afternoon. There's a constable stuck by every lamp-post and every
second person we meet between this and the palace yard is an obvious
'tec.' It will get on his nerves presently. I say, these foreign scoundrels
aren't likely to throw something at him — are they?[50]

and:

"If he will insist on beginning a revolution!" murmured the Assistant
Commissioner.
    "The time has come, and he is the only man great enough for the
work", protested the revolutionary Toodles. ...[51]

But the fisheries bill and the "revolutionary Toodles" are a parody
of everything else here, the central destroying moment, as if to say
one must peel layer after layer of anarchy (under respectability)
until one reaches the heights of respectability, to find not anarchy
or revolution, but its parody, its pretending to be such (false, but,
of course, an anarchy of another sort). There is only here an
absurd voice and comment on this "imperfect world" — "Be lucid,
please", ruling out all compassion, and all understanding. The
Professor speaks of madness and despair; and passion, the only

[49] *Ibid.*, p. 125.
[50] *Ibid.*, p. 126.
[51] *Ibid.*, p. 126.

saving virtue, is mocked by confusion and insanity; Sir Ethelred is a revolutionary; and the other pole of the novel, anarchy and disorder, is mocked by pomposity and condescending respectability. The novel is parodying anarchy itself, its great theme.[52]

The comedy of *The Return*, *Outpost of Progress*, and *The Secret Agent*, then, suggests a total context of disorder, chaos, anarchy, delusion, and stupidity. Conrad, like his Mr. Vladimir (self mockery — the mocking of Conradian comedy) roams seeking subtle connections, incongruities, and non-apparent relationships — a stiff automaton railing against the passion of his unpassionate wife and defending a life without passion with passion, two children in a heart of darkness, and a lot of corpulent men playing at revolution and counter-revolution, supported by rich matrons, wooing in shady shops, seeking links with the worlds of Sir Ethelred, the police, the anarchists, and the embassies. Everyone seems to have his orange striped sleeping suit in these works. This is a bitter and non-innocent comedy, a comedy after the Fall. The people in these works are automatons who are mechanized and dehumanized, in a scheme of rigid actions and relationships. That every gesture of Allan Hervey is caught in a mass of mirrors is the appropriate figure for this, and one remembers the opening of *The Return*, where every gesture is duplicated and reduplicated, not in mirrors, but in actuality, because Hervey is one of a mass, each member of which acting as every other member, symbolized in the slamming doors of the train. Like the comic characters of *Heart of Darkness* and *Lord Jim*, the characters of *The Return*, *Outpost of Progress*, and *The Secret Agent* seem completely dehumanized (the comic form given to their actions signifies their dehumanization, as their lack of freedom), making their passions, beliefs, and sentiments all the more laughable. Moreover, the comedy is one of false appearances

---

[52] This is not to say that its theme is not anarchy — it certainly is — but the anarchy extends even to the level of artistic consciousness. One peels off layer after layer and finds more and more disorder and at the very core is the symbol for order used as a parody of disorder, and thus becoming, itself, disorder, through this parodying. But this also happens to what seems to be the only real order in the novel — artistic ordering — the novel's only counter-value. The problem is — how far reaching is this theme of anarchy, is it everywhere, in every possibility, and how are we to take it, once we see it.

and of sham gestures — a grotesque vision of fallen worlds where the mockery pervades everywhere, making of every thing, even of theme and action, folly. The comedy of these works then is a comedy depending upon the entire situation, a pattern of ironies and relationships and sentiments.

5. VICTORY

Victory is Conrad's most pronounced and extended allegory.[53] The theme of the novel is ostensibly the pursuit of almost helpless innocence and uprightness by the almost helpless evil and malignancy — not quite though, for Heyst is hardly blameless. The reader might even take his clue as to the nature of the novel from the lines of Milton's *Comus* that introduce and serve as a kind of motto:

Of calling shapes, and beckoning shadows dire
And airy tongues, that syllable men's names
On Lands and Shores and desert Wilderness.[54]

[53] It is the allegory which causes many of the difficulties of the novel — Leavis has noted that the "antithesis of lust in Ricardo and woman-loathing in Jones on which the denouement depends has no irresistible significance in relationship to Conrad's main theme". Hewitt has also felt a discrepancy between paraphrased theme and the actual effect the novel has on us. Guerard considers the novel to be "very badly written and very roughly imagined", to be "an awkward popular romance built around certain imperfectly dramatized reflections on skepticism, withdrawal, isolation". This is the problem. The allegory suggests the satanic trinity — Ricardo is the serpent (Death, where is thy sting?) — he is also a cat and lust — but there is passion in Schomberg, Heyst, and others, and parodies of passion, Jones and Schomberg. A major theme seems to relate to passion and its purgation. One could say that evil is viewed as a surrender to lower faculties and that the novel's bestial imagery indicates this. But the major problem is not focused on Heyst's passion in relationship to Lena. In other words, the allegorical Three are externalizations of Heyst's indifference, but as passion, which they really are or represent, they are externalizations of nothing *clearly* present within him. It is true that one could argue for repressions, but the idea of detachment and Heyst senior pervades too much and confuses. Also it can be said that Jones is afraid of women because woman shall destroy the serpent — the devil — but his mania seems almost, if not completely, a mocking of passion, absurd and exaggerated in gesture, paralleling Schomberg's lust and uxoriousness, also mocked. Structurally the weight is on passion. The allegorical structure is unclear — confused — suggesting two opposing themes, or hints of themes. There is inadequate merging. The allegory in its obvious form clashes with some strong underlying suggestions.
[54] *Comus*, 11. 207-9.

lines which ought to imply something of the nature of the temptation which is to follow.

There is a significant use of symbolism in this novel and there is
a "reduction of almost every character to a single symbol and function".[55] Jones, Ricardo, and Pedro can be regarded as "almost allegorical manifestations of evil",[56] possibly a satanic trinity of Satan,
Sin, and Death. Mr. Jones can be recognized as a modern version
of the devil, cutting a genteel and decadent figure.[57] He is evil,
"restlessly evil in the manner of a devil and taking a devil's delight
in planned cruelty and ruin".[58]

The most obvious case for this allegorical identification comes
from the novel itself. The arrival of the three on Heyst's island is
described as myth-like in terms of a legend of amazing strangers
"who arrive at an island, gods or demons, bringing good or evil
to the innocence of the inhabitants".[59] There is further reinforcement of this identification when Jones in speaking to Heyst states:

A man living alone with a Chinaman on an island takes care to conceal
property of that kind so well that the devil himself —[60]

a reference, I suppose, to himself. In fact, one notices in other
places in Conrad where allegorical or semi-allegorical figures are
suggested that a frequent use of the word *devil* (as Curse or allusion)
occurs. This is the case with *Chance*. In *Victory* this can be seen
early in the novel when Schomberg comments to Ricardo: "Ah,
well. I've been already living in hell for a few weeks so you don't
make much difference."[61]

Jones is Satan; he personifies a "singularly noxious brand of
evil",[62] and is portrayed as an "insolent spectre on leave from

[55]   Marvin Mudrick, "Conrad and the Terms of Criticism", *Hudson Review*,
VII (1954), 422.
[56]   Robert Penn Warren, "Nostromo", *Sewanee Review*, LIX (1951), 375.
[57]   Robert W. Stallman, "The Structure and Symbolism of Conrad's *Victory*",
Western Review, XIII (1949), 152.
[58]   E. K. Brown, "James and Conrad", *Yale Review*, XXXV (1945), 278.
[59]   *Victory* (London, 1948), p. 228. All subsequent references to *Victory* will
be to this edition.
[60]   *Ibid.*, p. 382.
[61]   *Ibid.*, p. 115.
[62]   Katherine H. Gatch, "Conrad's Axel", *SP*, XLVIII (1951), 102.

Hades".[63] The fear he inspires is satanic and is described as a "superstitious shrinking awe, something like an invincible repugnance to seek speech with a wicked ghost",[64] which is closely related to his mesmeric abilities. Heyst feels his strange power, and:

His very will seemed dead of weariness. He moved automatically, his head low, like a prisoner captured by an evil power of a masquerading skeleton out of a grave.[65]

But, of course, the problem is meant to also be much of an internal one.

Jones then is myth-like and Satanic. He is the fallen angel or its suggestion when:

Having been ejected, he said, from his proper social sphere because he had refused to conform to certain usual conventions, he was a rebel now, and was coming and going up and down the earth. As I really did not want to listen to all this nonsense, I told him that I had heard that sort of story about somebody else before ... then he said:

"As to me, I am no blacker than the gentleman you are thinking of ..."[66]

Ricardo also gives himself away when he comments: "You boys don't know who I am. If you did —!" and, expressing his gambling credo, he states: "I would play them for their souls."[67]

Thus Jones and company seem non-human and allegorical and a bit like the officers of the *Patna*, in that they seem to exist in a morality context. The important and focal point of *Victory* is the test between Lena and Heyst on the one side and the three on the other. Ricardo feels that "this is like no other job we ever turned our minds to", and Jones reiterates this when he says, "I have a peculiar feeling about this. It's a different thing. It's sort of a test." Moreover, Samburan is a stage, isolated and elevated, like *Patna*'s deck, as that is imaged. And this stage is the world and man's being, and the task "of Heyst and Lena is the labor of mortal man and woman to establish a barrier against the inroads of evil. The bridge built of old by the satanic host from Hell to earth touches the jetty on Samburan, and Schomberg revenges himself on Heyst

---

[63]   *Victory*, p. 116.
[64]   *Ibid.*, p. 121.
[65]   *Ibid.*, p. 390.
[66]   *Ibid.*, p. 317.
[67]   *Ibid.*, p. 149.

by pointing the way for the ancient emenies of the human pair —
evil intelligence, lust, brute force. ... "[68] Conrad uses Edenic symbolism during the final struggle, symbolism which reinforces the
allegorical nature of the struggle between Heyst and Jones. Lena
in a sense is asking: "Death, where is thy sting?"

> She had done it! The very sting of death was in her hands; the venom of
> the viper in her paradise, extracted safe in her possession — and the
> viper's head all but lying under her heel.[69]

In *Victory* Conrad repeats what has been in part done elsewhere —
burlesque is associated with representations of evil and an allegorical suggestion. This burlesque is so much associated with Jones
and company that they must often be thought of in terms of this
alone. Ricardo is like the second engineer of the *Patna* (and Donkin
in *Nigger of the Narcissus*), especially when he curses the sun (further
implications of the satanic). He is the absurd and noisy scoundrel,
braggart and braggadocio, "a pasteboard figure overdrawn to the
point of caricature", and a man who cannot be taken seriously.
In almost every grimace he shows and in almost every sound he
makes, there is an element of the ridiculous:

> The secretary ... emitted a grunt of astonishing ferocity as if proposing
> to himself to eat the local people[70]

and:

> The secretary retracted his lips and looked up sharply at Schomberg, as
> if only too anxious to leap upon him with teeth and claws[71]

and as he is leaving Schomberg, "he showed his teeth to Schomberg
over his shoulder".

Then there is Ricardo's manner of speaking. He discourses
about gentlement and knives:

> You can't tell how a gentleman takes that sort of thing. They don't lose
> their temper. It's bad form. You'll never see him lose his temper —
> not for anybody to see, anyhow. Ferocity ain't good form either — that
> much I've learned by this time, and more, too. I've had that schooling
> that you couldn't tell by my face if I meant to rip you up the next minute

[68]   Wiley, p. 155.
[69]   *Victory*, p. 399.
[70]   *Ibid.*, p. 101.
[71]   *Ibid.*, p. 112.

— as of course I could do in less than a jiffy. I have a knife up the leg of my trousers[72]

and:

It's a more handy way to carry a tool than you would think ... Suppose some little difference comes up during a game. Well, you stoop to pick up a dropped card, and when you come up — there you are ready to strike, or with the thing up your sleeve ready to throw. Or you just dodge under the table when there's some shooting coming. You wouldn't believe the damage a fellow with a knife under the table can do to ill-conditioned skunks that want to raise trouble, before they begin to understand what the screaming's about, and make a bolt — those that can, that is.[73]

Equally ludicrous are his utterances on work:

Work be damned! I ain't a dog walking on its hind legs for a bone; I am a man who's following a genteman. There's a difference which you will never understand, Mr. Tame Schomberg.[74]

Ricardo, who is willing to risk anything at any time (in his affirmation of manhood which is not doghood, but which is really cathood), hates the "tame" ones with a vengeance. And he feels the injustices of the world, for he has been wronged, and the world is filled with "hypocrits". He especially feels the injustices of Heyst's treatment of Morrison:

It's the very way them tame ones — the common 'yporcrites of the world — get on. When it comes to plunder drifting under one's very nose there's not one of them that would keep his hands off ... It's the way they do it that sets my back up. Just look at the story of how he got rid of that pal of his? ... What was all that coal business? Tame citizen dodge; 'yporcrisy — nothing else. ... [75]

And when he speaks to Lena:

You and I are made to understand each other. Born alike, bred alike, I guess. You are not tame. Same here! You have been chucked out into this rotten world of 'yporcrits[76]

and:

Blamed 'yporcrit. ... He's one of the tame ones ain't he.[77]

[72] *Ibid.*, p. 136.
[73] *Ibid.*, p. 136.
[74] *Ibid.*, p. 146.
[75] *Ibid.*, pp. 264-5.
[76] *Ibid.*, p. 297.
[77] *Ibid.*, p. 297.

He has an obsession concerning this "yporcrisy", and his hatred shakes every bit of his cat-like frame (and gets his back up in a cat-like manner). He in his braggadocio bravery has a curse for the unjust world and its tame populace — "Hang them for a beggarly, bloodless lot animated cucumbers" — and when he curses the ape-bear-dog Pedro, he screams in the same fashion:

Aha dog! This will teach you to keep back where you belong, you murdering brute, you slaughtering savage, you! You infidel, you robber of churches! Next time I will rip you open from neck to heel, you carrion-eater! Esclavo![78]

In fact, in everything he does and says Ricardo is the exaggerated clown villain of low comedy.

Not only does much of the burlesque in *Victory* center around this character, but there are also several scenes of low-comedy slapstick. Heyst's first sight of the strange trinity is one, and they announce their arrival on Samburan in a fairly grotesque manner. Pedro is the last to show himself — he is hirsute and black — and he grabs the secretary and throws him from the water pipe. This is followed by what would appear to be a brief battle of the clowns, where Ricardo shows all the bravery he boasts of. He grabs a heavy piece of wood, and with all his force brings it down upon the ape's head. A second blow dispatches Pedro from the water-pipe, and Ricardo gives the creature a tremendous kick. But the poor, hairy beast is an ingrate, and Ricardo screams that the ape ought to kiss his hands for all his kindness:

Yes! you ought to burn a candle before me as they do before the saints in your country. No saint has ever done so much for you as I have, you ungrateful vagabond. Now then! Up you get.[79]

a ridiculous ending to a fantastic vision. The ape has hit the cat, after which the cat has hit the ape, and they fall about, before the cat rises to lecture the ape on his ungratefulness and the cat's saintliness.

Other burlesque or comic elements are the trunk which Jones and Ricardo carry about with them, a trunk loaded to its very brim

---

[78]　*Ibid.*, p. 231.
[79]　*Ibid.*, p. 240.

with weapons. The villain enters literally armed to the teeth. It announces that he is, of course, a villain, a desperado. And there are reasonings and speculations as to the location of Heyst's non-existent loot — futile and absurd speculations.

Finally there is Mr. Jones himself and his great mania, his misogyny and its rhetoric, which some critics find rightly implausible as it was possibly meant to be, a mania parallel to a mania as exaggerated as that of Ricardo concerning "'yporcrits" and "cucumbers". Jones (for Satan, although as Satan he may always recall his punishment and the role of woman) is too easily excited at the mention of woman, and he engages in too many over-elaborate metaphors and figures of speech to be taken as plausible. When Schomberg mentions the all-girl orchestra (eighteen women), Jones sings out in dismay and looks about him as if the plague had taken to Schomberg's hotel. He swears violently and at Schomberg for daring to bring up such subjects. Thirty-six women might have caused a total collapse and catastrophe. But in actuality one will serve. The scene at the novel's end, which is emphasized as the great test between Satan and Heyst, is broken into and disturbed by Jones' rantings when he discovers the presence of Lena on the island and the betrayal of Ricardo. At that moment, evil and its suggestion, as external force (or symbol for internal one), completely disintegrates into burlesque and the irrationality[80] it represents. The scales seem tipped and Heyst's great opponent seems no more and no longer very formidable,[81] for Jones is frozen by this information of Lena's presence, and he joins Ricardo and Schomberg in their monomanias, cursing all lovers of women, all low class, "amorous cusses", and literally leaping out after his feline secretary:

"On the track! On the scent!" he cried, forgetting himself to the point of executing a dance of rage in the middle of the floor.[82]

[80] Which is possibly in keeping with Conrad's identification of evil with irrationality through animal images — but animals have cunning and intelligence — Jones here becomes clear insanity, taking wild shots, and dangerous in that respect, but not very dangerous.

[81] Of course, all this hinges on Ricardo's lust which betrays — so one can say lust destroys, Satan as well as men. But something is not too clear: that Satan should be the victim of lust rather than its dispenser, a fact which makes the allegorical apparatus of this novel problematic.

[82] *Victory*, p. 389.

At the very moment of crisis, Jones cries out in classical imagery and allusion the absurdity of his entire self:

"Behold!" the skeleton of the crazy bandit jabbered thinly into his ear in spectral fellowship. "Behold the simple Acis kissing the sandals of the Nymph, on the way to her lips, all forgetful, while the menacing fife of Polyphemus already sounds close at hand — if he could only hear it! Stoop a little."[83]

nonsense syllables except in the comically mad imagination of the fading Mr. Jones.

Conrad has then made extensive use of some of the elements of burlesque here creating a comic image for three characters who supposedly form a satanic trio. Burlesque is made part of the crisis and test. There is much that is exaggerated and buffoonish in the plottings of Ricardo and Jones, and Heyst's first vision of the three — Jones, Ricardo, and Pedro — is accompanied by the savage but frenetically absurd blows and groans of a remarkable Punch and Judy show. Even the rejected lover Schomberg in his passion almost chokes himself in his vehemence, and every time he thought of Lena, "He spat. He choked with rage — for he saw visions, no doubt. He jumped up from his chair, and went away to flee from them perhaps."[84] His fight with Zangiacomo is of the same sort, snapping, rolling on the floor together, chasing each other all over the house, with "doors slamming, women screaming, seventeen of them, in the dining room; Chinamen up the trees ... ".[85] After a second fight, these "two offensive lunatics" ride off together in the same gharry to save expenses.[86]

Evil in this novel seems clearly to be comic and burlesqued. But more than this, the burlesque, as elsewhere, indicates a correlative for disorder and a reducing of disorder to a recognizable symbol and order — what has been called elsewhere a ritualization of disorder.

More than in any other work of Conrad, bestiary images dominate. Ricardo is the cat-serpent; there are bears, dogs, apes, and

---

[83]   *Ibid.*, p. 393.
[84]   *Ibid.*, p. 61.
[85]   *Ibid.*, p. 48.
[86]   *Ibid.*, p. 50.

jaguars. The major action, despite the stated and reiterated theme and problem, seems focused on passion, and a purification and a purgation of it. Structurally, the novel only makes sense this way,[87] for in its earlier parts we have a lot of Schomberg and in its latter parts we have a lot of Ricardo — who is also death. Even Jones' mania is passion. And there are undercurrents of this theme in the relationship between Heyst and Lena. At the risk of seeming too schematic, one can relate the doublings and the parallels of the novel into fairly clear patterns — Jones, who does not act and who is silent, is the evil side of passion as mind, passion perverted and *disguised* as mania; Heyst, who cannot act and who is silent, is the good side, and passion *disguised* as cynicism or idealism of a sort; Ricardo, who speaks out and acts (as does Lena), is open and revealed passion, but its evil side; while Lena is open passion, and its good side. In Lena and Ricardo, passion is drawn into the open, revealed, united, and purged through the act of the taking of the sting, or knife, or phallus.[88] But the final aspect or purgation is the *liebestod* — death by fire for Heyst, and, its evil analogue, death by water for Jones. Nevertheless, the expense is great; the purgation involves total destruction and annihilation. In reference to the allegorical structure, Ricardo and Pedro and evil are imaged in terms of the animal; they are reduced to a ferocious, elemental, and animalistic intensity and pose, and this is supplemented by a relationship to lust. Schomberg's lust for Lena sends them to Samburan, and Ricardo's lust for Lena destroys his partnership with Jones, causing the wildish catastrophe which follows. Evil becomes madness and impotence through lust. And it becomes the irrational. The animal is lust, and the elemental, signifying no restraint, is the irrational — the association is made and carried through in the complex of the actions of Ricardo and Jones in relationship to Lena. The evil of the novel, which is to say the destructive passion, is a disorder of a sort analogous to the life-boat disorder of *Lord Jim* or the central station fire disorder of *Heart of*

---

[87] Passion is a theme in *The Return, Heart of Darkness, The Secret Agent, Chance, Nostromo*, etc. — especially in relationship to the theme of restraint.
[88] See the work of Moser.

Darkness. When Ricardo hits Pedro, when Jones is on the track, when Zangiacomo and Schomberg toss and tumble before tree-loads of frightened Chinamen; we are given the implications of all animalistic fervour and lack of control. And we are given the implications of lust. That which is mocked, made absurd, is passion, both open and disguised. Schomberg chokes and turns blue; he is a mocking of passion; and Ricardo rants and Jones leaps — each a monomaniacial passion towards some goal or desire. The evil is comic; its passionate side, ridiculous.

Victory has no Marlow, and no young captain-narrator-artist being initiated, and the problems and complexities and ironies associated with these characters are avoided. But if Conrad is to show us that all the trouble lies within Heyst,[89] is Heyst's indifference and world-weariness, this still does not explain why externalizations (or allegorizations) of these things were necessary, and if one argues that the externalizations were necessary to show us the quality of the internal danger in terms of a moral world, then, why, one wonders, make this external symbol so filled with folly — if it is to be the great test, it should then seem like the great test. Possibly, we are to be called upon to see what indifference is (but why would that disorder be imaged in terms of the comic?), its qualities and aspects, and the comic has this function.

Comedy and burlesque in *Victory* are part of a Conradian process of undercutting and undermining. This is most effective when it undermines pretensions and gestures and values of a society. But when it seems to undermine a theme, as in *Victory*, or in *Falk*, it is problematic. In *Lord Jim*, the undermining of a theme may be the novel's theme, but here there are no tensions between oppositions, no failures of judgment as theme, no pivotal narrator. The

---

[89] Ostensibly, his detachment and aloofness, more possibly his unknown passion which leads him to destroy his passion, or possibly which his aloofness and coldness, upon a recognition, pushes him to destroy. In any case, one is left with nothing at the novel's end. The allegorical form suggests Adam's combat with Satan, but Adam suffers from detachment and indifference, inability to act, and Satan is passion and madness, and so one sees an allegorical combat, but one does not see clearly how Heyst as conscious man shall fit into this combat.

undercutting has been transferred to Conrad's mind until it does aesthetic damage. The paradoxes are the same — burlesque which clarifies and defines also dodges and evades — the "necessary" symbol for disorder is also a mocking of that disorder, not only as disorder, but as part of a theme, as if to say one should not be too concerned.[90] And as an allegorist, Conrad can show us evil as part of a morality play through burlesque, but he can also show us not to respect this evil. The problems arising out of this device and its use in *Victory*, while also problems appearing earlier in Conrad, are in *Lord Jim* and *Heart of Darkness* integrated into a theme and an action, still remaining problems, but only as those whole themes and actions are. And this device is part of something occurring within Marlow. Comedy is a clever dodge — but in *Victory*, there is all dodge — the dodge seems to become all-pervasive — there is too much allegory, stiffness, blithe optimism and other very indicative inadequacies. The external is too much and too far separated from the internal; there is no sense of perplexity and confusion universalized (only the confusions of an artistic failure), no *tragic sense*, which pervades *Lord Jim*, for instance.

---

[90] The totality of *Victory* seems to be directed towards a theme of passion, for otherwise Schomberg and Ricardo are luxuries that perhaps should not have been permitted; and each part of this theme is mocked, the theme proceeding and developing by serious and mocking perspectives. Miltonically, Satan is a wall-leaping thief who runs with the four-footed herd. But a balance is maintained, and a real danger is felt. Comedy (in *Paradise Lost* — I assume the parallels to *Victory* to be obvious) is only a minor aspect, a way of seeing Satan's falseness and disorder, but not a way of saying he is so absurd that he is no threat. In *Victory*, however, there is no balance; the danger within is not clearly focused in terms of the external symbols — it is given an improper correlative — there is too much comedy. *Victory* is quite Miltonic — it is Miltonic to belittle evil and Satan through comic juxtapositions, to show disorder through comic burlesque — as in the war in heaven — but there is a balance between inner and external evils, and a danger is felt and perceived. But in *Victory* inner conflict as articulated clashes with external forms and symbols. Furthermore, Satan in *Paradise Lost* is given heroic stature (proven false) so that we can see that from one view he is false, but from another, in the eyes of men, he is not. There is no grandeur in the evil of Ricardo, Jones, and Pedro — no separation of views and no inner portrayal of them. So a belittling process here is much more destructive, destroying the problem and allegory itself. Unfortunately, an image and a traditional device can be two-sided — to a work's harm.

6. CONCLUSION

What one might call Conradian comedy can be broken down into
uses and types, dependent upon such factors as whether the novel
or tale employs a narrator-protagonist, a narrator, an omniscient
narrator, whether it deals with romanticism and romantic illusion,
or the profounder problems of men facing evil in its various forms
and manifestations. This comedy can be found elsewhere besides
in the works already discussed (there are elements in *Shadow Line*
and *Chance*, but they are not major enough to require discussion,
and the "comic opera" elements of the former work have been
treated by Haugh), but it is in the works considered that its presence
is clearest, and these works seem to contain the major aspects and
types of this comedy, and the major problems that go along with
its use.

The various uses of this comedy (its various forms being burlesque, slapstick, reduction, and so on) might be finally presented as
follows. That a comic image in relationship to an incident aboard
the *Patna* or the quality of activity at a central station in the Congo
suggests a metaphorical function seems reasonably clear. In the
case of *Lord Jim* implications are revealed and levels are added to
the original level of interpretation of Jim's fall, dream, experience.
Relating to a tradition and having literary reference, mean burlesque and "sordid farce" serve to suggest or reinforce the hint
of allegorical structure, implying in part the structure of a kind of
morality play. And as part of character, this comedy serves to
imply modes of perception and their limitations, suggesting in relationship to the transformations within the novels where Marlow
is important an illusion and an ambiguity central to these works.
Marlow's illusions relate to our own. And we also end in perplexity.
There are further illusions of significant tests, significant experiences, what we make of certain things. This is what I think *Falk* and
Youth are really about. Either the comedy itself is an illusion or it
is that which is used to reveal an illusion.

The comedy serves in certain cases to relate to the creation of the
structural pattern of a given novel or tale, and it creates further
thematic possibilities, as in the case where it hints at an anti-

journey, or, at least, demands of us that we not take what Marlow says at face value. And the comic image in the case of a novel like *Victory* suggests a transference from a character named Marlow to an omniscient narrator-author, and a total work. Without Marlow, a complexity and ambiguity and two-sidedness as theme becomes narrowed into a rather simplistic allegorical suggestion. Yet, if a comic image or slapstick farce or burlesque meanness is given importance here, without a rich context of ambiguities; if comedy which is reductive becomes an essential part of the creation of the novel's "satanic" threesome and their arrival and end on Heyst's island; then we can argue that we get an image of disorder, a reinforcement of allegorical structure, and perhaps a metaphor for a condition of Heyst's being. But we also get thematic confusion (between passion and indifference), allegorical confusion and ultimately doubts about the very significance of the threat and test whose significance has been continually urged upon us (and the comic image in part contributes to this urging).

So there are essential differences. But certain things remain associated with the comic of a certain sort, and it is possible to say that Conrad in some of his novels and tales associates low comic images with characters who embody some form of evil (or who represent a form of evil, or evil), with his villains, and also with certain other characters who are weak, impoverished, lacking in humanness, reason, awareness, or imagination, men for whom civilization essentially means the policeman on the corner and the delivery of mail. And of course these characters cannot be divorced from certain kinds of situations. All this was some sort of a starting place. But it was not possible to have this as a place of termination. Perhaps ultimately one might be able to interpret a meaning or meanings out of this common element as it is subjected to its variations, so that the variations would tell us something reasonably clear about the common element, The slapstick applied to the officers of the *Patna*, to the "pilgrims", to Jones, Ricardo, and Pedro, to Kayerts and Carlier is the common element. The variations are what this book has been about. The question must still remain: what happens when one, from the point of view of a single element, places alongside each other *Heart of Darkness*,

Victory, or *Falk*. There is a reason or reasons for the common element. There must be a reason or reasons for the variations and transformations.

Finally, it is possible to suggest, if one might desire some concluding schema, that Conrad's great works such as *Lord Jim* and *Heart of Darkness* (and perhaps a work like *Falk* is a better work than it is usually considered to be — it is one of Conrad's works most needing careful re-examination and re-evaluation) combine, in their uses of "sordid farce", "knockabout clowning", "burlesque meanness", and "horrible comedy", the two kinds of works which have comic images and Conradian comedy. For, on the one hand, works like *Youth* and *Falk* either relate the comedy to something within a narrator-character, or suggest an analogous undercutting of theme, form, and so on, on the level of the total work striving to create certain obscurities and ambiguities (at least on some level) in these works. On the other hand, in the narratorless (and great works) such as the *Secret Agent*, or *Outpost of Progress*, an emphasis is placed upon mechanical men in an empty world. In *Heart of Darkness* and *Lord Jim* there are states of being, modes of perception, dreams, deceptions, the unconscious, struggle.

STUDIES IN ENGLISH LITERATURE

1. WILLIAM H. MATCHETT: *The Phoenix and the Turtle: Shakespeare's Poem and Chester's Loues Martyr*. 1965. 213 pp. Cloth.   Gld. 26.—

2. RONALD DAVID EMMA: *Milton's Grammar*. 1964. 164 pp.   Gld. 18.—

3. GEORGE A. PANICHAS: *Adventure in Consciousness: The Meaning of D. H. Lawrence's Religious Quest*. 1964. 225 pp., portrait.
   Gld. 25.—

4. HENRIETTA TEN HARMSEL: *Jane Austen: A Study in Fictional Conventions*. 1964. 206 pp.   Gld. 25.—

5. DOROTHY SCHUCHMAN MCCOY: *Tradition and Convention: A Study of Periphrasis in English Pastoral Poetry from 1556-1715*. 1965. 289 pp.   Gld. 30.—

6. TED E. BOYLE: *Symbol and Meaning in the Fiction of Joseph Conrad*. 1965. 245 pp.   Gld. 24.—

7. JOSEPHINE O'BRIEN SCHAEFER: *The Three-Fold Nature of Reality of the Novels of Virginia Woolf*. 1965. 210 pp.   Gld. 24.—

8. GERARD ANTHONY PILECKI: *Shaw's "Geneva": A Critical Study of the Evolution of the Text in Relation to Shaw's Political Thought and Dramatic Practice*. 1965. 189 pp.   Gld. 20.—

9. BLAZE ODELL BONAZZA: *Shakespeare's Early Comedies: A Structural Analysis*. 1966. 125 pp. Cloth.   Gld. 18.—

10. THOMAS KRANIDAS: *The Fierce Equation: A Study of Milton's Decorum*. 1965. 165 pp. Cloth.   Gld. 21.—

11. KENNETH HUGH BYRON: *The Pessimism of James Thomson (B.V.) in Relation to his Times*. 1965. 174 pp. Cloth.   Gld. 20.—

12. ROLAND A. DUERKSEN: *Shelleyan Ideas in Victorian Literature*. 1966. 208 pp. Cloth.   Gld. 24.—

13. EARL J. SCHULZE: *Shelley's Theory of Poetry: A Reappraisal*. 1966. 237 pp.   Gld. 29.—

14. CHARLOTTE BRADFORD HUGHES: *John Crowne's "Sir Courtly Nice: A Critical Edition"*. 1966. 183 pp. Cloth.   Gld. 23.—

16. BARBARA BARTHOLOMEW: *Fortuna and Natura: A Reading of Three Chaucer Narratives*. 1966. 112 pp. Cloth.   Gld. 17.—

17. GEORG B. FERGUSON: *John Fletcher: The Woman's Prize or The Tamer Tamed. A Critical Edition.* 1966. 223 pp. Cloth. Gld. 24.—

18. EDWARD VASTA: *The Spiritual Basis of "Piers Plowman".* 1965. 143 pp. Cloth. Gld. 18.—

19. WILLIAM B. TOOLE: *Shakespeare's Problem Plays: Studies in Form and Meaning.* 1966. 242 pp. Cloth. Gld. 28.—

20. LOUISE BAUGHMAN MURDY: *Sound and Meaning in Dylan Thomas's Poetry.* 1966. 172 pp., 11 spectograms. Cloth. Gld. 21.—

21. BEN H. SMITH: *Traditional Imagery of Charity in "Piers Plowman".* 1966. 106 pp. Cloth. Gld. 14.—

22. OVERTON P. JAMES: *The Relation of Tristram Shandy to the Life of Sterne.* 1966. 174 pp. Cloth. Gld. 21.—

23. LOUIS TONKO MILIC: *A Quantitative Approach to the Style of Jonathan Swift.* 1967. 317 pp., 56 tables, 15 figs., folding key. Gld. 34.—

25. BRADFORD B. BROUGHTON: *The Legends of King Richard I: Coeur de Lion: A Study of Sources and Variations to the Year 1600.* 1966. 161 pp. Cloth. Gld. 20.—

26. WILLIAM M. WYNKOOP: *Three Children of the Universe: Emerson's View of Shakespeare, Bacon, and Milton.* 1966. 199 pp., portrait. Cloth. Gld. 22.—

28. SOPHIA BLAYDES: *Christopher Smart as a Poet of His Time: A Re-Appraisal.* 1966. 182 pp. Cloth. Gld. 24.—

29. ROBERT R. HODGES: *The Dual Heritage of Joseph Conrad.* 1967. 229 pp. Gld. 27.—

30. GEORGE R. LEVINE: *Henry Fielding and the Dry Mock: A Study of the Techniques of Irony in His Early Works.* 1967. 160 pp. Gld. 20.—

31. ERIC LAGUARDIA: *Nature Redeemed: The Imitation of Order in Three Renaissance Poems.* 1966. 180 pp. Cloth. Gld. 20.—

34. ROBERT DONALD SPECTOR: *English Literary Periodicals and the Climate of Opinion during the Seven Year's War.* 1966. 408 pp. Gld. 40.—

MOUTON — PUBLISHERS — THE HAGUE